Hanno

under the bridge
new writing from northumbria

edited by Penny Smith

A Centre for Northern Studies Publication

First Published in Great Britain by
The Centre for Northern Studies
School of Humanities
University of Northumbria
Newcastle upon Tyne
NE1 8ST

2000

The copyright in each of the stories in this collection remains with the original copyright holder.

This is a work of fiction and any resemblance to actual events or persons living or dead is unintentional and purely coincidental.

Printed by Athenaeum Press Ltd
Dukes Way
Team Valley
Gateshead
NE11 OPZ

Cover designed by Department of External Relations, University of Northumbria

This book is sold subject to the condition that it shall not, by way of trade or otherwise, be lent, re-sold, hired out, or otherwise circulated without the Publisher's prior consent in any form of binding or cover other than that in which it is published and without similar condition including this condition being imposed on the subsequent purchaser.

ISBN 0 9511 4725 0

Contents

Penny Smith   **1**
   Introduction

Celia Bryce   **2**
   Sheets

Bob Cooper   **8**
   All We Know Is What We See
   The Day Frankie Nearly Died
   Where You Hear About Class

Philippa Collingwood   **11**
   Touching Eighty
   Rollerblading At Three O'Clock On A January Afternoon

Chris Powell   **13**
   Take a Tin Soldier

John Barfoot   **18**
   The Right Woman

Chrissie Glazebrook   **35**
   Schrodinger's Wife
   Epilogue

Josephine M. Fagan   **37**
   El Sabor de Miel

Marlynn Rosario   **45**
   Always The Indian
   Missing
   Travelling By Numbers

Sue Vickerman 48
   The Exorcism

Karen Laws 59
   Pompeii

Kriss Nichol 60
   Hyacinth Days

Brighid Morrigan 61
   Louise

Janine Langley McCann 63
   A cake fit for a skin-bird

Jo Morris 65
   Silent Running

Valerie Laws 70
   Maas en meisjes
   Why me?
   River blindness

Joanna Curtis 72
   Turning Soft

Liz Sampson 77
   Shearing

Eileen Jones 78
   The Stray
   Off Line

Pru Kitching   **80**
    Small pebbles by the river

Andrea Russell   **81**
    Mouse

Jo McCullock   **85**
    Camper

Marie Dobson   **96**
    The Taste of Friday

Patrick Murphy   **99**
    Gulf Crisis

Caron Henderson   **100**
    Alice In Sunderland

Adam Fish   **108**
    Travel
    City of Seahorses

Katherine Zeserson   **110**
    The Mother's Face

Matthew Pacey   **114**
    A Good Reputation

Gareth Rowe   **120**
    Upon First Looking Into Raymond Carver

Gary Player   **121**
    A Star Is Born

Chris Coles   **121**
    Two Englynion

Angela Readman   **122**
    Goose

Shauna Mackay   **133**
    Hush

Joe Quinn   **138**
    Tobhta an Da Mhail: The Ruin with Two Rents

Peter Baker   **139**
    Coach Touch
    Modern Love

Kevan Ogden   **140**
    Grief

Introduction
Penny Smith

Bridges have a particular significance on Tyneside, they are part of the mental as well as physical landscape. Bridges take you to the other side and far away from home. Or they bring you back again. Lean over the edge (your knuckles white but it's worth it) and down below there's the exhilarating flow and pull of the tide, debris and depths, the anticipation of not really knowing what to expect next.

Look at the writing in this collection and it's like watching the flow of water under the bridge. It is full of energy and life. There are depths and reflections and places where it might be risky to go. Above all there is movement. Many of the pieces are finished while others are still in progress — and the careers of the writers are in progress as well. All of the contributors are past or present students from the Creative Writing MA at the University of Northumbria and this is an opportunity to watch new and exciting writers at work.

The North is a good place for writers and for writing. Maybe it's something to do with the bracing climate. Maybe it's the long history of hard graft, craftsmanship and innovations in industry. More likely it's to do with the richness of everyday language. This is border country and the native words don't lie easily on the page — they are tough and untamed and those who work with them need to be able to experiment and to feel joy in the raw energy of language.

That said, you won't find a 'school' of writing here. The variety in style and subject and setting is wide. What you will find is poetry and prose which is powerful, accomplished and challenging. You'll also find names that you'll come across again in the future, and when you do you'll remember where you saw them first: under the bridge.

Celia Bryce
Sheets

That day, it was as if the whole world fell in. The wet sheets tumbling down, encasing my father and me in a blue-white world where, for a moment, nothing could get at us and time stopped.

The cool white dampness fell on our heads and we fumbled about pulling the sheets this way and that. I drew my hands across his face mummified in sheet, felt his nose, his ears, big and pressed close into his head as I smoothed the sheet like film over it. His soft mouth moved beneath my hand and his warm breath seeped onto my skin. I knew he was smiling.

And then we burst into uncontrollable fits of laughter and sat in our sheet tent, tears streaming down our cheeks. We had not laughed for so long. And I would have given anything for that moment to last because it was as if then all the bad things had never really happened, and that my father was himself again. But then Hilde next door came to rescue us, spoil it all and untangle the mess, peel us apart like tights from a tumble dryer. I ran to my bedroom and cried.

My bedroom was my world. In it an altar, on the mantlepiece, yellow plastic egg cups filled with blue bells and dandelions, cut short to fit and set on each side of Our Lady who smiled at me and had plaster roses growing from her feet.

From my bedroom window I could touch the sycamore tree, open the window and take one of its huge leaves in my fingers. In summer, they paddled against the glass, waking me with a gentle stroking as if not only touching the glass but my cheek also, and in my imaginings it was something my mother would do.

Here I made plans, wrote letters, which lay for weeks not sent. They piled up in the drawer beneath my bed where only I could find them. Letters to my mother.

My bedroom was the place where I made decisions. It was where I decided to strip all the beds and wash the sheets.

'But why?' my father asked.

'Because.'

'That's no answer.'

'Because they're dirty and need to be stripped off the beds and put in the washer and done. That's what you're meant to do.'

He turned back to his newspaper.

'Dad.' I took the newspaper away from him, crossly. 'Come on. The sun's out. They'll dry in no time.'

He looked at me and took my head between his hands, kissed my hair. 'For a twelve year old you're terribly bossy.'

'I'm not twelve.' I was thirteen. He had forgotten my birthday. I had forgotten his. Somehow we seemed to have mislaid everything. As if all things important had been put away in a drawer for safe keeping.

It took us a long time to work out the washing machine. My mother had left instructions in big looped letters and we sat looking at them as if it was a foreign language, as if each word needed digesting, making us fall into deep silent thought. We sat there for some time just looking at her writing, unwilling to leave it. Then my father put on the kettle, made coffee for him and tea for me, and we sat again, saying nothing.

Everything my mother had written had order to it. She had written as if instructing a small child, not an adult. There were things to do first, and things to do next. There were colours which could be washed together and colours which could not. But there was no mention of individual items, such as knickers or sheets.

'I suppose we just bung them in and be done with it,' my father eventually said.

'But we don't know which number to put them on.' I felt useless and stupid to have thought up such an idea in the first place.

'Let's just guess,' he said. 'They're white, aren't they?' His voice now had an edge of irritation to it. I nodded, trying to muster up some courage but my stomach was beginning to turn.

'I'll go and strip the beds then,' I said.

He let out a long breath as if he had been holding it in. 'No, I'll do it.'

'Tell you what,' I continued briskly, 'You do yours. I'll do mine.' I marched upstairs.

It took me some time to rearrange everything. The animals had to be taken off the bottom of my bed where they lived, and put in a row under the window, facing out and in order of size. The biscuit packet under my pillow still had biscuits in which needed to be eaten. And the pillowcase would not come off the pillow without tugging hard. It was the first time I had ever done it. It had never looked so difficult before.

Then it was all done and I carried my bundle along the landing to find my father sitting on the edge of the bed with the sheets rolled up on his lap. He did not notice me. His thumbs stroked the fabric, slowly. Big thumbs, clean fingernails. Always clean. My stomach tensed up. The sun would go in if he sat there for too long and then the sheets wouldn't dry and we wouldn't have anything to sleep in, except different ones. And I didn't want different ones.

'Dad?'

He looked up at me as if he had forgotten my name, as if somebody else's girl was standing there, not his. And the feeling that this idea was a very bad one began to creep over me, that the whole thing was just too difficult. I should never have suggested it. What did it matter that we slept in dirty sheets? It didn't matter at all. Not really.

I wanted to take them out of his hands, put them back where they belonged, so that at least this part of us would be the same. So that we could keep this one thing when everything else had been stripped away, leaving us raw, leaving us deposited somewhere else, not home. Not the home we used to have when my mother was in it and we were whole.

But the beds were stripped and piles of linen lay in our arms and the sun was getting higher, which meant it would come back down again and nothing would be dried unless we did something soon.

They were in at last.

My father sat in the kitchen with his paper in front of him. He was looking at the words but not reading. His eyes moved over the page from top to bottom and then started all over again, as if he couldn't quite understand what was written there. As if it was one long complicated crossword clue.

I went back to my bedroom, sat and listened for the low hum of the washing machine, barely there really, imagined each twist and turn of the drum, each revolution carrying our sheets, washing away the dirt and everything that was there.

The animals sat beneath the window, with their shining bead eyes and fur, big and small. Presents. Mostly from my mother. The last one a Possum. I looked at Possum and remembered her words, her hands as she gave him to me, her eyes on me as I unwrapped his soft little body.

And suddenly it was too much to bear, all of this. I raced downstairs into the kitchen and to the washing machine. Tried to pull the door open. My bewildered father looked at me.

'Get them out, Dad. Get them out,' I shrieked. 'I don't want them washed. Please, Dad.'

'Hey, hey,' he said quietly, putting his big arms around me, pulling me close to his chest. 'It's nearly done now,' he said. 'Finished.'

But I was inconsolable and sobbed until he took me on his knee and stroked my head. 'Come on, love, don't cry.' He rested his head on mine and for a long time we sat, me hot and sweaty with grief, and my father's face pressed into my hair.

'We need to rub the line with a cloth,' I told him later.

'OK. You find the cloth. I'll wipe.'

'And the pegs are under the drainer. I think.'

'Yes, probably. Off you go. There's a good girl.'

The first sheet went up. My father smoothed it across the line and I held it off the grass. It was from his bed. A big double sheet. White. He put a single next to it and then the other double. The line went to the bottom of the garden and so did the sheets, the pillowcases and the pegs. All different colours. Plastic, like toys.

'Who was the man who fought the windmills?' he asked, taking the clothes prop and holding it in front of him like a javelin.

'Don Quixote.' I said, pleased with the smile on his face. Pleased that maybe I had put it there.

'That's me, then,' he said and aimed the prop at the line.

It was in position. We both hoisted it up until the sheets hung like sails from a mast. Standing beneath, looking up into the sun we watched them as the wind began to catch and lift the corners, balloon out the middles. And then the prop broke and the line snapped. Everything fell on top of us. And Hilde came out.

'This is terrible,' she was saying, her English heavily weighted with her native German. 'All of this will have to be washed again and you are laughing?' She shook her head at us, amazed. 'I will take them,' she went on. 'They will be ready tomorrow. Nice and clean again. Oh, look at the mud.' It had stuck to the sheets like iron filings to a magnet.

'No,' my father was saying, laughing still. 'It's all right. We'll do them again.'

'I will do them for you,' Hilde said, her face full of concern. Dismay, even, at the two sillies attempting it themselves. How incompetent, how lost we were.

I got up and brushed down my clothes hoping that my father would win the argument, but seeing the laughter dry up and his face returning to its empty shell, could not stand it any longer and ran upstairs to my room. There was no way, now, that we would be able to put the sheets back on our beds.

I sat and looked at my altar, wiping my eyes with toilet paper. While my mother was here, the altar was kept trimmed and neat with flowers. Every day, new flowers and sometimes sycamore leaves when I forgot to pick something from the garden. I would find small leaves, something which would not overturn the egg cups.

And each night, I lay in my bed and said a prayer to Our Lady. It wasn't a prayer really, it was just a request, knowing that while we all kept tired smiles on our faces and laughed and talked sensibly about the future which held only two of us, our only wish was to stay in the past, which held three.

I would have to look for other sheets. They were in the cupboard at the top of the stairs and smelled of being there for weeks. Months. There was no soap powder smell, no smell of the person who had put them there in neat folded piles. But I held them to me anyway, because her hands had been there once and that was all there was.

We made up the beds in silence, my father and I. Blue sheets on my bed, and yellow on my father's. His bedroom looked brighter, I thought, and one day, I knew, we would have to move the clothes from my mother's chair.

Back in my room I started to put my toys back in their places at the bottom of the bed then decided against it. The smaller ones could go on the mantlepiece. Possum too. The bigger ones could remain under the window. I might move the dressing-table too. It would look like a new bedroom and the thought of something new made me smile. I emptied the flowers from the egg cups on the mantlepiece. They had been neglected and the stalks were brown and dry, the water long evaporated. I wiped out the egg cups with some tissue and put them in the drawer of my dressing table.

I looked at Our Lady for a long time wishing that she would move, or weep tears. Something. To prove that she was worth all the trouble I had taken in keeping her altar. But I knew she would do nothing, and for the first time noticed how her smile was only painted in place, that underneath, the sculpted mouth was not smiling. Not really. And it seemed to me that all the time I had spent on her had been wasted time, like trying to blow up a burst balloon. I held the statue in front of my face, remembering those occasions when I had kissed its painted cheek, wondering how I could have been so stupid.

I opened the drawer under my bed and lay the statue face down on top of the letters my mother would never read. There would be no more letters, I decided. Writing to a dead person was like kissing the cheek of a piece of painted plaster, like believing in a smile that was not really a smile. Stupid.

Bob Cooper

All We Know Is What We See

And everyone in front of Fenwick's Christmas window turns round
from Gepetto at his workbench and the island with its donkeys

when, with all the passing children of half-term, we're speechless as we watch
the clown on his 2 metre unicycle, who, instead of juggling more balls,

now puts a gloved finger to his lips, and Shhh we all say as he smiles
then wobbles a little as he takes off his clothes, his red nose and over-size shoes,

and, with his whole body painted gold, steadies himself then completes a headstand
where he tries to balance, his willy pointing to each shoulder then, at last, to his chin

when he lifts his hand up to his crotch, tugs it off, and turns the right way up
and our eyes focus elsewhere — a woman, after all that deception - a woman

who stretches her arms up like the Northern Goldsmith's statue and begins circling round
while the newspaper seller, the soldier who'd repeated *Buy a Poppy, Buy a Poppy*,

the pensioners in groups, the children who watch as if they understand, all cheer,
and is she a lover, wife, mother, a customer complaints manager, is she hot,

could she, without being naked, be a barrister, or stand talking after church, is she cold?
All we know is what we see: gold skin, grease paint, a curly wig and white gloves,

as she leaps down, pulls on her clothes, then wipes off her black tear,
and pushes her wheel through the crowd like a pram, like Pinochio's long neb.

The Day Frankie Nearly Died

It's six in the evening, the streetlights coming on,
though the Cathedral clock struck three minutes ago,
and I've already been to The City Vaults,
had a Tetleys, bought 20 Silk Cut,
then glanced in at The Blackie Boy,
where Tommy behind the bar said he hadn't seen you,
and there was Frankie near The Imperial,
pissed as usual, lighting a roll-up and trying to sing,
but he didn't see me so that was OK

while the Marxism Today guy crossed over again —
the old one with the pony-tail and tartan D.M.s
who I'd try to ignore outside The Beehive
until he mentioned oppression and I'd got onto Stalin,
though he hadn't heard of Akhmatova or Mandlestam,
and he'd interrupted, said poetry was unproductive,
but, still in full flow, I'd switched to the Prague Spring,
flowers in the gun-barrels of tanks, then Jan Palach —
while Frankie sang on, *to brighten up even your darkest night* —
and I was reading Baudelaire when Palach curled up in flames,
Les Fleurs Du Mal for the first time, and a woman's hair
as rich as tobacco that I'd loved to have smoked, inhaled —
and now hearing again that hard-left tone as Frankie relights his tab,
holds his bottle like a microphone and continues to croon,
You just call out my name while the finger-wagging starts
and Frankie shouts over to me as the shoving begins

when this police car pulls up and they get out,
pull on their caps, then stand each side of Frankie —
and I'm sure they're going to lift him — but this Socialist guy
gets hold of the Safeway Cognac, steps to one side,
turns his back, stuffs a hanky in the top,
tips it, lights it, though no-one else notices —
then throws it at the car, and it doesn't explode
until Frankie falls over — or is he pushed —
then everything flares, purple blossoming light
and I see you over the road, running to them,
wrapping your coat round Frankie's hair,
shouting something so loud at the night
and our faces, like the Vltava, frozen over.

Where You Hear About Class

Under a Canaletto print sky over the Tyne two lads in Berghaus jackets,
front-to-back baseball hats, eat hamburgers, suck their fingers:
*When I can I'll get into an XR3i, Blaupunkt speakers, leopard-skin seats,
drive that tammi cunt out to the coast and fuck her stupid.*
His mate lights a cigarette, stretches his neck, gobs down at a seagull,
I'd go for a GTI and Chantelle. While talking through a Cosworth and
Suzanne
they share a can of coke, watch a guy and a girl screwdriver a white Series
5.
Each kid punches the air as the car scorches past, handbrake turns and is
gone.
Six seconds. Real wicked. Then the other yells too, *Real class.*

Philippa Collingwood

Touching Eighty

At the Sycamores Rest Home
Relations are encouraged —
Except sexual ones like me.
So Matron, you quiet us, interrupt us

With a knock at this door.
Everything alright Mr Robert? — Only
We prefer our guests
Downstairs during the day.

And all three of us know
None of the locks have keys,
But we're both sure the door wedge
Smuggled in my bag will hold.

My breasts are now pendulums
Of a grandmother clock
But even at your age
You still like to know the time.

My nipples are now loose buttons
Hanging by a thread but you still enjoy
Sewing them back on.
With your replacement hip

We've had to adjust a bit —
We're both over sixty-nine,
Past missionary work
But you still fit me to a T

And arthritic hands need exercise.
My friend Joan, touching eighty,
Still plays tennis twice a week.
Isn't she marvellous?

And Arthur's admired for riding
Miles on his bike at eighty-five.
They've never stopped. Why should we?

Rollerblading At Three O' Clock On A January Afternoon

Choosing the middle
Where the tarmac's smoothest,

I keep passing another woman
Exercising in trousers too.

We share the same colour hair
Though she's past dyeing hers.

Only six wheels on her walking frame.
Neither of us have brakes.

We've both had to find
Somewhere quiet and flat,

Endure other people's stares.
We share smiles.

*It's more fun
With wheels on your heels!*

She's not much more
Than twenty years ahead.

I lean forward,
Skate faster before the light goes.

Chris Powell
Take a Tin Soldier

Lucy creates exquisite things out of metal. Tiny objects spun tissue fine. She thrusts a dull gobbet of ore into the fire and heats it to precisely the right temperature. She teases out a gleaming thread, a fragile thread, tough enough to weave into a gossamer blind or a beekeeper's veil. A month or so ago she took to fashioning insects. My favourite is a red-eyed damselfly; its wings are a fretwork of silver so delicate you could poke a hole through with your finger. Coral beads are its eyes and its body a scrap of topaz culled from the jewellery makers' scrap bank. Red-eyed damselflies are found south of the Wash in England, rarely further north, although they can be seen in southern Scandinavia. I have never seen one. I looked them up in the Collins Guide, hoping to impress Lucy with my knowledge. When I saw her in February, however, she had switched her attention to dragon-flies, they were larger, she said, less fiddly and she liked the paradox implicit in the name which suggested fire-loving creatures, and their habitat, which is water.

In March, I was preparing some sketches, hoping to win a commission to illustrate a collection of fairy-tales for a small, specialist publisher. I envisaged gaunt line drawings, monochrome washes, a hint of the skull beneath the sequinned skin. A copy of Hans Christian Andersen's stories lay open on my desk. When Lucy phoned, I'd been flicking through, looking for the one about the tin soldier and the ballerina because, when I was a child, it made me cry.

Take a tin soldier; cast him on to the hearth. Watch him relax in the enveloping warmth, then curl up into a self-protective knot against the flames. Soon he will melt, metamorphose into a shrunken lump the size and appearance of a shrivelled walnut. It may be his heart that is left, it may be something else. Only you can decide whether it is worth preserving.

'He's gone,' she said. 'The bastard's finally, irrevocably, gone.'

I took it she meant Aeshna. Lucy and Aeshna had lived together for seven years. He was a photographer. They were an item in every sense; if you could buy the perfect couple off the shelf, you would choose Lucy and Aeshna. He was olive-skinned with darkly hawkish burning eyes, she translucent as the Snow Queen. Arm in arm, a Roman chariot coupled to an Icelandic sleigh, they raced into private viewings, first nights, intellectual soirées, generating little flurries of artistic sparks, electric ripples of cultural disagreement and aesthetic debate. Just before Christmas he walked out on her and moved in with a younger model. Everyone expected it, but no-one believed it.

'Gone where?' I said, 'What do you mean?'

'He's going to marry her,' she said, 'have babies. He wouldn't marry me.'

'But you didn't want him to, did you?'

'That's not the point,' said Lucy. 'I thought you of all people would understand that.' And she slammed the phone down. I didn't really understand why she said me of all people, but her words gave me a quick burn of pleasure.

Dance lightly across the coals *en pointe*, if possible, to minimise the risk of scorching your feet. Carefully remove what is left of your tin soldier using a pair of long-handled tongs.

A couple of days later, she phoned me again. 'I'm sorry,' she said, 'you're my friend. I shouldn't have lost my temper. But who does he think he is? To dump me and hitch up with that child, it's such a cliché!'

'Perhaps he's been reading too many Hollywood gossip magazines,' I said, weakly.

There was a long silence. I held my breath. Then Lucy gave a deep sigh. 'Perhaps,' she said, 'Why don't you come round?'

So I went to her workshop, as I do, every time she summons me. I am a moth to Lucy's flame. I can't help it.

Once you have removed the heart from the fire, allow it to cool. It will turn black. Don't worry, that's because of the oxides, it is to be expected. Keep it in a jar; I like to use the sort that once held Mrs Elswood's pickled cucumbers.

I knocked when I reached Lucy's place and went straightaway to open the door, which is always open. Only this time, she had left the chain on. I called through the chink and after a while she appeared. Her face was flushed and her hair a little wild. I love to see her like that, hot from the making process, she glows like a fire opal.

The workshop was full of rainbows. She was fabricating copper bowls. Small, perfect bowls. She was beating them with a tiny hammer. This was very unlike her usual style.

'That looks like hard work,' I said.

'It's therapeutic,' she said as the hammer pirouetted and pulsed across the surface of the metal, 'and the copper is still quite malleable.'

'Ah,' I said, 'that's what Aeshna wanted, of course, a softer option.'

'Of course,' she echoed me precisely and I regretted saying that.

'What happened to the dragonflies?'

She pointed to the ceiling. They hung in a tinkling cluster from lengths of fishing line, cavorting like drunken trapeze artistes, below an open skylight. The light through their wings explained the rainbows. Each one was gorgeous. Graceful. Sublime, like everything Lucy made. But I wanted to set them free.

Lucy continued to work in silence. Just as I could no longer bear to watch the way her hair fell in damp strands across her forehead and her long fingers flickered up and down the stem of the hammer, she looked up.

'Do you want to have a go?'

'Can I?'

'Of course. I will teach you the whole process, so you understand.'

'What are they for?'

'To hold the pieces of an ex-lover's heart.' She laughed at the expression on my face, 'Aeshna,' she said, 'has a very tiny heart.' I was thinking about my tin soldier. She took me over to her workbench. She bent over me, 'Listen very attentively,' she whispered. I breathed deeply and let her arms guide me.

'Take a strip of copper. Silver would be best, but it is too precious for this task, and besides, you are not ready to use silver. Measure it. Hold the scriber, this pointed metal tool is a scriber, in your right hand and mark out to the nearest millimetre the distance between what you want to see and what you know is true. Make the lines fine, not too deep but deep enough to tell.'

A film of machine oil floated on the surface of her skin, perfuming the air as her blood warmed it. She led me to the guillotine. We placed the strip of copper beneath the blade and she let it fall. When she turned out the lights I began to have difficulty breathing.

Lucy passed me a pair of goggles. 'The annealing process begins,' she said. She reached for the gun. It was idling in its cradle, slack, a nonchalant blue flame licking around the end of the nozzle. Lucy's eyes were bright, brighter than I'd ever seen them. She pulled her goggles down and primed the gun. It leapt in her hand and a tongue of fire whooshed out of the end, roaring. She took my strip of copper in her tongs and held it in the flame. Many kinds of subtle siftings down, shifts of balance, displacements and alterations took place as each molecule in my body aligned itself with every other, unable to resist the fierce heat. I began to soften. That is what happens when your molecules align. The flame skimmed my skin which sea-changed iridescent, blue, green, silver, oil on water, watered silk, then as the fire rampaged to its apotheosis, to darkest, deepest, brightest red. Just as I fell into the dark hole in space where solid objects liquefy and begin to flow, I opened up, peeled back like a pomegranate and sighed into blackness.

'Plunge the hot metal into the pickling bath,' said Lucy. 'See, as it rapidly cools on hitting the water, the surface of the copper is oxidising and turning black. The solution in the bath is ten percent sulphuric acid, which is slightly stronger than malt vinegar, and will loosen the black deposits. Scrub with carborundum powder to remove any lingering traces of soot. Now you are ready, soft and clean enough to face the press-forming machine.'

She led me over and laid me down. This is what a press forming machine does: you lay your softened copper strip over a steel template into which a hole corresponding to the circumference of your bowl has been punched; you heap damp sand on top; cover this with a heavy metal block; swing the handle until the clamp falls pressing the sand down on to your copper, forcing it through the template to form a perfect bowl. The intense pressure re-scrambles the molecules and the shape becomes rigid, ready to be filed, beaten, finished-off.

'Do you see?' She said, 'That's what I do.'

I saw. Lucy, I love you, I wanted to say. Turn me into a dragonfly. But I was afraid that she would laugh, so I said nothing.

Lucy and I are still friends. I visit her workshop when she is in town and occasionally we meet over candlelight in Aeshna's wife's bistro. He takes very few photographs now, but seems content instead to wait at table and look after their child. He has grown plumper, more plastic, his eyes no longer blaze confrontationally.

A smart London gallery exhibited Lucy's bowls; she has become well known in different circles, quite a celebrity. Among the cognoscenti, I am told that it is quite the thing to display a collection of Lucy's minimalist copper bowls on a glass shelf next to the fire, where their surfaces will reflect the glow from the flames. She has had a string of younger lovers: hard flesh, soft in the head, red-hot in bed, she says; we laugh about them sometimes.

And I am illustrating fairy stories. My drawing of the Snow Queen is based on Lucy, of course, although I will never tell her that. I'm having to work quite hard to keep to the original stark vision. My images keep developing trelliswork, lattices, elaborate tracery. The ink smokes across the page like a damselfly's wing. But I'll get over it. Take a tin soldier, toss it on the fire, plunge your bare hand into the flames, pluck out the heart.

John Barfoot
The Right Woman

I like looking at women. To see without being seen: that's my ideal. Unfortunately, most of them want contact, engagement. They think it's creepy if you just want to look.

Finding the right woman. That's always been my problem. If it hadn't been for the party I might still be searching now. It would all have happened anyway, I suppose — loneliness getting harder to bear, pressure building up — but it would have been slow. I don't know how far gone I'd have been by then. The party brought things to a head.

I still don't know why I went. I find it's best not to have friends when you live alone. But the new people had a flatwarming. They invited me. They invited everybody in the building. I think it was the surprise. I like to plan in advance, but being asked right there and then, on the doorstep, it didn't seem possible to say no.

I regretted it when I actually got there, but it was too late by then. Someone shoved a drink into my hand, said something I couldn't hear because of the noise, and then cast me adrift. It was frightening. There were lots of women and I couldn't keep my eyes off them. I felt vulnerable, as if there might be a point when they would notice I was looking at them and turn on me. As a consequence, I drank a lot, much more than I'm used to. I've never drunk to excess, mainly because I don't like the feeling of losing control, but on that night it was something to do, something to be engaged in to avoid standing out. All I remembered, later, was that when I was least expecting it, when I was just starting to feel at home with the female bodies all around me, the sort of distanced intimacy I most enjoy, several of the men grabbed me by the arms and ushered me out. They were surprisingly rough. One of them shouted something at me and the others laughed as the big front door banged shut. And standing there swaying in the cold night air, I was instantly drunk. I staggered, had to steady myself against the iron railings. Nearly fell headlong down the steeper steps to my basement.

I had not been exposed to so much talk and laughter, so much loud music, so many people performing, since I was a boy. Back then, I would sneak partway down the stairs and watch from the shadows, my eyes always on my mother: her bare shoulders, her moving hands, her head thrown back in laughter. She would never see me. It was my father who would notice and send me back to bed. But sometimes, without saying anything, he'd sit with me, the two of us watching in silence, and if anybody came up to go to the bathroom we'd stay out of sight, retreating round the corner of the wide landing until they'd gone. And there were some nights when the party seemed to get wilder and wilder, like a phrase of music approaching crescendo. Her dancing would turn reckless, abandoned. I would feel an unbearable tension, as if something momentous was about to happen. It never did, but something of that feeling of breathless expectation was with me now, as I locked myself into my flat. So much so that I found myself wandering from room to room, putting lights on, peering carefully into the bright empty spaces. I didn't know what I was looking for, but it felt as though something was eluding me, something coy, always just out of sight. I really felt a presence of some sort, and on the theory that whatever it was might venture out when my attention was elsewhere, I left all the doors open and pretended to watch television. There was nothing on any of the sixty channels I sampled, so it wasn't long before I switched off and watched the dot diminish. When it was gone I looked at my CDs. I didn't feel like listening to any of them, not after all the noise upstairs. They were already in alphabetical order, so I counted my books, neatly shelved according to height, and one or two jarring transitions between spine colours made themselves obvious. While I carried out the necessary minor rearrangements, I looked over my shoulder at the open door. There was nothing there.

That was when I thought about all the couples in the house above me.

They'd be going to bed. In rooms stacked over my head, women would be undressing, just like my mother all those years ago, when the last guest had gone. Hands reaching behind her back to undo the clever little clasp. Legs turning gracefully inward so that the welted tops of her stockings could be unfastened. Arms raised high to shake nightwear down over her naked shoulders.

The weight of all I imagined happening above me now was forcing hot waves to radiate from my stomach and moisture to ooze from my forehead. I knew it was only a matter of time before I was sick, so I went to the bathroom and sat on the edge of the bath. It was quiet in there and I soon dozed off, but I couldn't control the spinning with my eyes closed. I slumped down beside the toilet and breathed heavily for a while, waiting for it to happen. Soon enough, dry heaving began. Painful retching took over. Something squeezed up powerfully from my stomach, hesitated, and was there at last. Sour, lumpy stuff. Forcing itself out through my mouth and nose. Splattering against the toilet bowl. Dragging my intestines after it.

If only. If only I could vomit my body empty. Liquidise it's contents and eject them. Puree my brain and flush it. Scour my head clean. Start again, hollow. Hollow sounded peaceful. I blanked out for a few seconds, and when I came back, I was kneeling before the toilet, head turned sideways, the rim of the bowl cold on my cheek. I was empty, staring at a few square inches of floor behind the sink, and I was seeing what was there with a clarity that seemed somehow terrible. That was when the idea of her first came into my life. That moment of merciless lucidity, squeezed from me by the party, that was what forced me to really grasp the import of the assemblage of rubbish that had piled up behind the sink. I realised that it had been familiar in the corners of my vision for some time now, had somehow retained its shape despite all the forces of air disturbing the bathroom floor. Now, all at once, I began to understand what it might mean.

A loosely woven clump of hair and grit, in the chance form of a tiny harp. That was what I saw. What I experienced was recognition.

Next morning it was still there, that tiny trap for dust, and pieces of skin, and pile shed from the towels. But last night's hangover was thudding massively in my head, and in the gloomy light admitted by the tiny frosted window high in the bathroom wall, it seemed less significant. My certainty wavered. By the time I had endured a taxing day at work and a dispiriting journey home, the matter had been driven almost completely from my head, and she might have ended there. Stillborn. But something — perhaps only curiosity — made me look again as soon as I got back. My heart lifted. The cluster of scraps had visibly grown. Its greater depth and solidity were obvious. The resemblance to a harp had gone. Now, miraculously, it looked more like something huddled in on itself.

There was no wavering after that. My first act each day was to check behind the sink. And each day I saw its substance increase as it captured particles from the steamy atmosphere of the bathroom. As with clouds, the tiny individual transitions that marked it's mutation from one shape into the next were too subtle to be noticed. But like a cloud, it changed constantly. I had not had meaning in my life since my father had driven my mother away. Now I realised that it was slowly returning. I had a reason, a purpose, an agenda outside myself. Work became a nuisance that ate up a large part of each day, but because my new interest had caused many long-standing problems there to be consigned to the back of my mind, it had become, paradoxically, easier. A good thing, because my fascination with the tiny creature behind the bathroom sink was crowding everything else out. My sense of anticipation became almost unbearable.

And so it went until, one morning, I found myself looking at what appeared to be a curled-up embryo. It was made mostly of my body's own detritus and there was no hard outline, no definite boundary where it ended and the world began, but the resemblance was startling. I was shaving at the time, leaning to one side with the razor at my face to check on its progress, and when I saw the outsize head, the stubby limbs, the knobbed spine curving down into a tiny tail, my hand jerked and I cut myself badly.

By the time I'd managed to stop the bleeding the sink was full of red trails and the floor around my feet was covered with splashes the size of pennies. I cleaned the sink up first, and when I knelt to mop the tiles I found the pink comma shape stuck at the edge of a blood-spot. At first I assumed that the air currents set up by my movements had blown it out from behind the sink, but closer, down on hands and knees, face hovering, I saw that it appeared to be absorbing the blood. This close the embryo-form was obscured by the disorderly network that made up its body, but as each individual hair, skin-flake and twist of cotton slowly turned red, the humped shape began to come back into focus. I watched fascinated as the splash of blood steadily diminished and the embryo grew more substantial, more there as a real, living thing. When the blood was gone it lifted as if a breeze had taken it and moved on to the next red pool. It was grazing.

I watched, fascinated, as it fed and drifted, drifted and fed. Soon, the vestigial tail disappeared. The limbs became more shapely. A neck grew between the torso and the head. There was rapid random movement behind the translucent eyelids. Veins pulsed near the surface of the skin.

I cried. Tears fell on it and around it. It was as if I had given birth to this creature, budded it from my body. I was feeding it with my own substance: blood, and now salt.

I sniffed and lifted my hand to wipe my face, and the downdraft sent it scudding across the floor, back behind the sink. In the shadow there it looked more random again. The tiny human shape was still visible, but I had to turn away and look out of the corner of my eye to see it.

I dressed and went to the phone box on the corner. I don't have a telephone myself. There's no-one to phone me. I'd feel vulnerable anyway. I like to prepare before I speak to people.

All the way down the street I coughed to roughen my voice, turned my collar up and hunched my shoulders to get in character. The sweat and ammonia smell inside the box helped. And the echo.

I told them I couldn't come in, I had a cold. They said I sounded awful. Said not to hurry back, to make sure I was fully recovered before I thought of returning. Told me to take care of myself.

I didn't feel good about it. I don't like lying. But then again, I've never been off sick before. I can't see the point. Most of the people I work with would probably say it was about time I stayed away and stopped making them look bad.

Back home, I picked at the dark ropy line on my cheek and dabbed some fresh blood on the floor near the creature. I took care not to make a breeze, but there was no movement anyway. It didn't look much like an embryo now, more like something that should have been swept up. The core-shape was still there, I was sure, but it was entangled deep in the network.

I tried again, carefully placing a droplet so close that it enveloped the end of a stray hair as it spread. There was a slight stirring, but that could have been me, displacing air. I reasoned that it would eat again when it was hungry.

I was right. When I looked carefully round the bathroom door for the hundredth time that night, at about seven o'clock, there it was, sitting in the middle of the floor like a smudgy charcoal drawing. I was prepared. I had my scalpel ready, the one I use to cut out images from books and magazines. The blade was new, still greasy from its waxed-paper wrapping and I was hardly aware of the sensation when it slipped into the flesh of my forearm. Blood welled and dripped. The creature seemed to rise off the tile into three dimensions. It rotated slightly and then drifted to the nearest pool. It's body began to fill out immediately, like a balloon inflating. The mouth, where the blood was being greedily ingested, was first, then a slow wave of colour revealed the rest, moving like a wash of paint in a cartoon, out from the delicate head, down the curled up torso, into the tiny bud-like toes.

When the pool was drained, it rose and drifted to the next. And the next. And the next.

The floor was clean. I lay down carefully and extended my arm so that the cut was near to where it had come to rest. Its eyes fluttered behind closed lids. Its nose flared. The flow from the cut was sluggish by now, clotting already, but bright fresh blood was still just visible in the lips of the wound. I closed my eyes, and a few seconds later, there was a tickling sensation. I looked down the length of my arm. It was lapping, lips fastened to the incision, tongue like a little bird's tongue as it moved in and out. I felt myself start to cry again, but took care to remain perfectly still. The tears rolled down my cheeks as it fed from me, moving slightly now and then in its contentment.

I fell asleep, probably only for a few minutes, and when I woke up, it was gone. My arm was aching. I inched backward until the area behind the sink was visible. At first all I could see was a big clump of hair and rubbish. But then, as my eyes adjusted, I realised there was no ambiguity this time. The fuzz-ball was merely the extended body, the unfinished edges. Cocooned in the centre was a large, healthy, pink embryo. Its thumb was in its mouth and the mouth was working gently.

Over the next few days my embryo came to full term. I fed it every morning and evening, opening new cuts each time so that the food would be fresh. After each feed it seemed to become more human, the scraps and waste of which it was composed less obvious. Protruding hairs were drawn back through the skin, millimetre by millimetre, and the bio-flakes and cotton-threads left behind fell away like scurf. On the day the boundaries of the body could clearly be discerned, like something brought properly into focus at last, I considered her born.

Yes, her. She was female. I had known it all along. I didn't name her because no name seemed adequate. She was she, pure and simple.

Having responsibilities towards another living being puts one's priorities into order like nothing else. This was a long term job, and I was going to have to do some long term planning. I wondered about paternity leave, but quickly dismissed it. Too many explanations would need to be given. Nevertheless, work owed me. I had given everything, now it was only right they give something back.

I bandaged my arm, dressed and went to the phone box again. It felt strange, being out in the open after so long. I felt like an intruder from some other dimension, only half corporeal, drifting ghost-like. I got some strange looks, but that wasn't surprising, I suppose. I hadn't shaved or washed for a week. Such mundane actions seemed inappropriate in the place where my baby was being born. I hadn't eaten much either.

Someone had been sick in the phone-box. I turned my back on the still steaming mess and dialled work. There was no problem. They understood colds took a while to shake off. They were having to reorganise after the recent management survey anyway, and my job description was in the melting pot along with all the others. Things were 'in a state of flux' at the moment. I was just as well out of it for the time being.

They were very kind. Concerned about my welfare. I wished I didn't have to deceive them, but I had no choice. I just said 'Thank you,' quite emotionally, and hoped that my sincerity would come through over the wire.

At the little Indian shop I dithered along the packed shelves for a few minutes and then settled on a 'high-energy/low calorie' diet preparation. It would be easier and quicker both to prepare and eat. There was no time to waste on unnecessary activities. I wanted to enjoy every moment of my baby's childhood.

The bearded Sikh man behind the counter looked at me searchingly as he put my purchases in a bag and took my money. My coat-sleeve pulled back as I stretched my hand out for the change, and his eyebrows went up when he saw the bottom edge of the bloodstained bandage. He said nothing, but his look made me feel that I had disappointed him somehow. I felt a vague anger start to smoulder. He wasn't my father. He had no right. When he said, 'Take care,' as I left the shop, I pretended I hadn't heard him.

The next few days, the days of her childhood and adolescence, were difficult for me. At first, I spent all my time with her, watching in wonder as the proportions of her body changed, making her head and trunk seem to decrease in size, her legs and arms to grow longer. I saw feet and hands become both stronger and more delicate, baby fat become lean muscle, fine baby hair thicken and spread to form a ragged fringe, above eyes that deepened hourly in colour.

But as she started to acquire more adult bodily characteristics, I felt less sure of myself. Her body was changing all the time, like a TV picture renewing itself constantly, and altering subtly with each renewal. She seemed unaware of this rippling mutability, completely unselfconscious of her nakedness, but I felt increasingly uncomfortable. One part of me wanted to continue to watch, but I instantly recognised a base impulse, the sort of primitive behaviour I have tried to suppress all my life. She was my child, after all.

In the end, I decided to leave it up to her. I imposed myself on her only at feeding times, and even then I entered the bathroom with head averted, closing my eyes as I heard the faint sussuration of her movement, the feather touch of lips on my flesh.

The rest of the time I sat uneasily in the bedroom or living room, trying to leave her the space I imagined a young girl needed to develop in. Any time she spent with me would be of her own choosing.

I will admit that I was disappointed when days passed — days which were the equivalent of years in her accelerated growth — and she did not come to me. Apart from our feeding sessions, the only times I was in her presence were accidental. She was still attached to the bathroom, the place of her birth, but during my restless wanderings around the flat, I would sometimes come across her in some other room. She would be looking uncertainly at furniture or light fittings, standing with her ear close to a ticking clock, rubbing the edge of a curtain between finger and thumb as if trying to work out its purpose. When she became aware of my presence she would smile shyly without looking up — she had never yet looked directly at me — and drift back to the bathroom. I would observe helplessly her burgeoning hips, her slim waist, the light fuzz of hair that was starting to appear on certain parts of her body.

On the morning I glimpsed firm, fully mature breasts as she knelt to feed, I decided it was time she had some clothes. I was reluctant to leave the flat, but I would have to go out soon anyway for more diet supplement. I didn't care for myself, but I had to keep nourished for her sake. She depended on me.

By this time, both of my arms and my left leg were covered in cuts. I sterilised the scalpel each time in boiling water, but I suppose it must have slipped my mind occasionally. The earliest cuts were beginning to fester and a faint smell was coming off them.

I took bandages from my home first-aid kit and wound them loosely around myself. Blood and pus seeped through in places, but my coat and trousers would hide that. I had still not washed — how could I when it would mean invading her privacy? — and my face was grubby with stubble. It could not be helped. Few took the trouble to see me when I was peering out from behind cleanliness and a diffident smile. Why should a slight change in the mask make any difference?

I called at the Indian shop first, sure that I would feel more legitimate if I went into Tracey Girl on the High Street with a bag of shopping already swinging on my arm. The bearded Sikh man was not there and I felt a surge of confidence as I gathered an armful of the diet supplement from the shelf by the window. However, as I dumped my purchases on the counter, he shouldered through a bead curtain with some cardboard boxes in his arms. He put the boxes down and took over from the young Indian girl who had started to serve me.

Again, he stared at me as he packed the diet food into a plastic bag. His eyes didn't leave mine, even when I looked down, and I felt he was taking in everything about me. My father looked like that sometimes. He'd ask gently about girls, girlfriends, and he'd ignore my protestations that I was happy on my own, only interested in some answer he seemed to find in my eyes.

'All right?' he said gently. I heard him, but I muttered 'Pardon?' and then pretended to drop my money. I took my time picking it up and feigned a coughing fit as I handed the coins across to him. Both of us noticed at the same time the dirt and grimy bloodstains on the back of my hand. He grimaced and turned uncertainly to the till. I didn't wait for my change.

Tracey Girl was quiet. Two young girls sorted casually through rails of hanging garments, talking and giggling, occasionally looking in the long mirrors and becoming very professional and serious as they considered the top or skirt one or the other held against her body. An equally young girl manoeuvred a pushchair through the narrow aisles between the stands and racks, trailed by an older woman with a burning cigarette protruding at right angles from an extravagantly cocked hand.

The tall woman behind the counter had a mobile phone to her ear, but she was already looking hard at me as she talked. I did not feel very substantial. Only the weight of the plastic bag I was carrying prevented me from floating away. The tall woman's scrutiny threatened to shred me into trails of mist. I nearly turned and left, but letting her go naked any longer would be wrong. I began to hurry around the store, adopting the persona of someone who knew exactly what he wanted and had no time to spare. Within minutes I had an armload of clothing. I made my way through the aisles to the counter and laid it all out in a heap, already tugging my credit card from my wallet.

The tall woman was still talking into her mobile. Now she said, 'Talk to you later. Something's come up.' She started to separate the garments and key their prices into the till, glancing up at me suspiciously as she did so. After two or three entries, she stopped and sorted quickly through the rest of the pile. 'Do you know these are all different sizes?' she said.

Size. Size had slipped my mind. It was too late now. I knew somehow that it wouldn't matter anyway.

'That's OK,' I said, head down as I pretended to rearrange the contents of my carrier bag. 'No problem.'

She said nothing, just looked at me for a second or two. Then she sniffed, and took up the next item, a pair of impossibly high-heeled shoes I couldn't remember choosing. The two girls were waiting behind me to be served and I heard them suppressing giggles. The girl with the pushchair and the older woman had turned their heads to look at me. The girl was chewing gum. The woman's face was hard.

'Hundred and seventy three ninety nine.'

I handed my credit card over and had to force myself to wait while the machine chattered and paused, chattered and paused. The women stared at me, dropping all pretence of politeness. I signed and hurried from the shop. I felt like a criminal, but as soon as I emerged into the open air all that fell away. I was loaded with bags. It was like camouflage. I had a right to be there.

As I passed the phone box at the end of the street I suddenly remembered work. Squeezing in with my bags I dialled the number. I told them I still felt a bit shaky. Would it be all right if I took my annual holiday now? Make sure I was completely well when I returned.

Haven't you had the letter? they said.

Back home I stepped over the pile of mail I hadn't bothered to look at and locked and bolted the front door. Nothing to do with me personally, said the letter when I found it. Or the way I did my work. Just Economies of Scale. Rationalisation. Downsizing.

At first I was scared. Although I appreciated the reassurance as to my personal worth, my stomach had seemed to fall out of my body at the thought that I was jobless. Set adrift. It took me back to the time when my father told me mother wouldn't be living with us any more. The same sense of fear and betrayal. Didn't they know that all the best management theorists saw work as more than just a means of making money? Didn't they realise I had needs as well as responsibilities?

Then I saw her through the open bathroom door.

She had matured fully during my absence, had become buxom almost. She was lying in the empty bath as if it was a giant cot, brow knitted as she gazed at the taps, trying to determine their function.

I shut the bathroom door quickly, ashamed of my weakness. They were apologising for setting me free when now was the time I needed my freedom most. In a way it was a relief. I knew some of the younger girls in the office felt uncomfortable with me. I could see it in their faces and in the way they pulled their skirts down over their legs when I was near. I tried to keep my eyes averted, but they dressed so provocatively. Occasional visual contact couldn't be helped. There was no lewdness in my interest. I simply found myself enjoying scattered moments of appreciation.

I wondered whether something had been said, whether that was why I was one of the ones let go. No matter. I should be grateful. I should thank them. She was going to need all my time. She would find that there was no harm in me.

That night I dreamed her into the clothes and into my bedroom. That's the only explanation I can think of. I'd knocked, and pushed the bags of clothing round the door, but when she didn't emerge from the bathroom, I knocked again and peeped in. The bags were untouched and she was standing up in the bath, tracing the pattern on the tiles with a finger. The long lines of her back and legs made my heart jump and I watched her for longer than was necessary before gently closing the door.

Disconcerted, I went to bed early. Despite the autumn chill the students next door were having a barbecue. They were sitting around a fire at the end of their dilapidated garden, grilling sausages in the flames, passing bottles round and talking quietly. I closed the curtains but a red glow filtered into the room from the gaps around them. It was restful. I almost felt I was part of their group, sitting a little further back from the fire, just listening, not bothering anyone.

At some point I must have fallen asleep so gently that I didn't realise it. I woke — in the dream, I think — to find her standing at the foot of my bed. She was looking at my pictures, the ones I cut from magazines and books.

The walls are pretty much covered now, but it's not like those scenes you see in films, where some dodgy mechanic wipes his hands on an oily rag in front of a wall covered with naked girls. My pictures are tasteful, nothing crude. In fact, most of the girls are fully clothed. And the images are treated. Manipulated. That's where my scalpel comes in. It's a giant ongoing collage, not a collection of pin-ups. Erotic rather than obscene. Most men don't see it — my father never did — but eroticism and pornography aren't the same thing. There's a difference.

She moved slowly along the carefully arranged interlocking images, seemingly fascinated. The glow from the fire flickered red on her side and hip, and threw a wavering shadow on the wall. I could have watched for hours, content, innocent, but after four or five minutes she walked purposefully to the door and left the room. I was disappointed, but I was also warmed somehow by the after-glow of her loveliness.

I must have drifted back into sleep then, because I remember waking abruptly to a harsh clicking on the tiled bathroom floor. This time I wasn't sure whether I had really woken up or was only dreaming I was awake again. The red glow had dulled a little, suggesting the passage of real time for the fire to die down in, but it's well known that dreams often incorporate stimuli from the real world.

Whether awake or still asleep, every detail of what followed was pin-sharp. Hyper-real, almost. The bathroom door groaned quietly where the hinges needed oiling, and the clicking changed to a few muffled taps. My bedroom door swung open and I saw her standing in the doorway in a pose I instantly recognised from one of the images on my collage: hands on hips, shoulders thrown back, one leg slightly akimbo. She was dressed like the young girls in the office: skirt that was little more than a tight band across her hips, tiny top that revealed her midriff and most of her chest, shoes that gave her another six inches in height. She was heavily made up, eyes dark pools, lips gash-like. I couldn't remember buying the make-up in Tracey Girl, but then I couldn't remember buying these immodest clothes either. My embarrassment had forced me to scurry around the shop, but it was curious that this revealing outfit was what I had come up with.

I kicked my legs free of the duvet and sat up, watching as she stalked aggressively into the room, hands still on hips, pelvis thrown forward by the high spike heels. She stopped at the end of the bed and adopted her pose. I couldn't help thinking that it was a pity the bed obscured my view of her legs, and as if I had sent a telepathic suggestion, she obligingly moved sideways. As she did so, the glow from outside lit her face and I saw that what I had taken for a provocatively direct stare was nothing of the sort. Her eyes were averted, as usual. She seemed to find the empty space at the other side of the bed more interesting than me. Fortunately, this made the next hour or so easier. I cannot deny that I felt a certain ignoble excitement at the prospect of taking in her body with my eyes without fear of being caught.

She began by demonstrating how well she had absorbed the images from my collage. There was silence except for the soft rustling of her clothes as she changed position, her body like a life-size projection of the tiny figures on the wall behind her. I would be lying if I said I was not stimulated by the display. I can only say that I allowed myself to watch for so long because the distance between us gave the illusion of some kind of chastity.

But when she moved closer, invading the zone that was my flimsy excuse, I started to panic. Suddenly, she was here, on the bed. She was kneeling above me, her skirt stretching and sliding. Her hands were touching my body: teasing; pulling and forcing. Her breath was moving over me, warm and damp on my lips and eyes. She was riding me, as if I were some kind of beast, and there were sounds — soft and wet and glutinous — contaminating the silence. And, most disturbing of all, she was trying for the first time to look into my eyes. I struggled, but she was strong, she had the advantage. I had to whip my head from side to side, and finally, reluctantly, close my own eyes, before I sensed her attention move away from me and felt her movements slow.

When she moved off me I turned over and buried my face in the pillow. After a while, the mattress dipped and tilted, and when I eventually turned my head for air, she was gone. I fell asleep in the mess she had forced me to make.

In the morning, disturbed by what had happened in the night, not even sure if it had happened, I tried to behave normally. But it was clear right away that things had changed.

For a start, the bathroom — her snug hut, her shelter, her sanctuary — was empty. A moth began to flutter softly inside my head. I ignored it and began to check the rest of the flat. She was in the first place I looked, lying on the couch in the front room, wearing a nightdress that left little to the imagination. She wasn't asleep — her eyes were fixed blankly on the ceiling — but when I sat carefully on the edge of the couch beside her, she closed them and went through the motions of waking up, stretching and yawning and arching her back. I think she did it for the effect she assumed it would have on me.

I pretended to be unmoved. I cut my right ankle, gathered some blood on my fingers and offered it to her. She licked half-heartedly but then moved up to my throat, nuzzling and nibbling as she had done last night, and again, disconcertingly, I sensed her eyes searching mine out. In an attempt to distract her, I opened a cut in my neck. It worked. She fastened her lips on the wound and began to suck and bite greedily. The sensation was erotic in the extreme, almost more than I could bear. I had to fight hard to retain control, and when she eventually fell away from me, sated, I lost consciousness.

When the moth brought me back, vibrating and trembling along the inside of my temples, I was alone. I staggered to the bathroom. She was not there. The contents of the Tracey Girl bags had been emptied in a heap. The floor looked like the bottom of a tart's wardrobe.

I turned to go and caught my reflection in the mirror. My neck was a red mess. My face was smeared with make-up a hidden observer would have concluded I had tried to apply myself.

There was movement at the edge of the mirror. I did not need to look. She would be standing in the pose she knew was my favourite: hands on hips, one leg akimbo, chest thrust forward. Her body would be an open invitation. I did not want to imagine her eyes.

So that was how it was for a time. She moved out of the bathroom and began to colonise the rest of the flat. Evidence of her presence was everywhere. A stocking draped over the back of a chair, knickers lying on the floor where she'd stepped out of them, a shoe hanging by it's high heel from the windowsill.

I avoided direct contact as much as possible during the day. I had to keep an eye on her to know where she was, and although I felt uncomfortable spying on her, that meant long hours watching her dress and undress, bend and move, sprawl and stretch. But as soon as the slow implacable pursuit began again and she started towards me, her eyes now blatant, shameless, I would withdraw silently into the nearest room, shut the door, and wait until she grew bored, or forgot her purpose. I had to grant access for feeding of course — I was still conscious of my responsibilities — but fortunately, our new feeding site seemed to distract her. Once I had opened a fresh cut on my neck, greed overpowered her predatory instinct. Her whole being concentrated on the slit she penetrated again and again with her tongue, and when she had finished, there would be peace for a while. The amount of blood I was losing was making me permanently tired, but I begrudged her none of it. I let my eyes rove her body while she remained comatose, and fondly remembered her origins, the days of her childhood.

Things were not so easy when the light began to fade and I had to go to bed. Night after night I would wake from lurid dreams to find her moving above me, her clothing rustling and scraping softly against my skin. There were no more red glows to illuminate her, and in the furry, breathing darkness, groggy with sudden awakening, I would be unsure where she ended and I began. I was permanently exhausted. Even the days became like waking dreams. And as those days and nights dragged on, twisting and coiling together like snakes in a pit, she began, gradually, to lose interest.

It was subtle at first, but I sensed it immediately. Her eyes became preoccupied again, dull, and they were starting to infect her body. Their boredom, their disinterest, their non-involvement, all spread slowly through her. Leaking, sinking, permeating. Down through her neck and torso, down into her legs. All the way down to her leather-shod toes.

I began to have nights free of her.

Feeding time became an obligation for me, a mere necessity for her.

And during the day, she spent hours standing motionless at the gap in the front room curtains, staring out at the street above.

She's gone now.

I watched through the door-crack as she pulled off the cheap clothes she was wearing. Pulled them off as if they were contaminating her, and left them in a heap on the floor. Her body was at the height of its maturity, a beautiful creation, worthy of the connoisseur's objective admiration. But she did not realise that every garment shed made her less interesting. Naked, she was nothing.

She moved towards the door and I scuttled out of sight round the corner of the passage. She walked — elegantly I have to admit, though without the tautness and power high heels confer — she walked to the front door. She paused with her hand on the lock, and then she turned, and for the first and only time, we were looking directly at each other. It was too late to duck my head back. Her eyes held mine. Two pinpoints of light in the gloom. I thought for a moment I saw reproach. An accusation of inadequacy. But then I realised that what was there was only the awareness of animals. Nothing human.

The lock clicked. Hinges creaked. A long blade of sunlight flashed once, and she was gone.

I hurried to the front room and peered through the gap in the curtains. A glimpse of naked legs on the steps. Her head turning to take in the sky. A hand trailing idly along the railings.

I closed the curtains. People can see into this room. They have no respect for privacy.

'Oh, my friend.'

He isn't packing the diet supplements. He's looking into my face, moving his head in little arcs, trying to catch my eyes. I pretend to be looking for something in my bag. I wish he'd just get on with it. I'm over her. I'm a new person. Weeks have passed. I've cleaned myself up, had an orgy of cleaning. Washed my hair, disinfected the wounds, scrubbed and scrubbed myself until everything's pink and healthy looking. Some of the wounds are inflamed, leaking a clear fluid. I've used flesh-coloured plasters on those. I don't want to disfigure my neck with plasters, but it doesn't matter. I've begun to experiment with make-up. I think I've done well. I think someone objective would even say that my face was pretty now, it's usual blandness enhanced by the effects of mascara and lipstick, foundation and blusher.

There's no need for further births. The rubbish on the bathroom floor is just that: rubbish. I'm looking inward now, and I've found her at last. The right woman. One who enjoys being looked at. One who will never leave.

At first I just let her be glimpsed at the door, had her retreat into the passage when someone passed by above. Then I allowed her out at night, walked her to the end of the street and back, letting her get used to the heels, the hand movements, the whisper of stockings. Now here we are in the full light of day. Our debut.

'Oh, my friend.'

He puts his hand on her shoulder. I shrug it off. Why do men think we appreciate their familiarity?

I throw some money on the counter and we flounce out with our bag of diet supplement. I let her hips sway, feeling the skirt tighten and relax against her silk-clad legs, tighten and relax. We've practiced for hours in the flat. I know what it looks like. I know he's looking at us. I don't care. When you've got the right woman nothing else matters.

Chrissie Glazebrook

Schrodinger's Wife

What he does up there is a mystery.
He's secretive. The door is always locked.
'Liebling,' he says, 'it's quantum theory',
though why he needs poor Heidi to concoct
a line on sub-atomic particles
is lost on me. He puts her in a box,
with litter made from shredded articles
by Einstein, pops in some cyanide, then locks
the lid. Inside, he tells me, there's a mass
of highly radioactive matter
which might decay, according to the laws
of quantum physics. Give the cat a
break, Erwin, or the RSPCA
might get a call (anonymous) one day.

He says the point of the experiment
is that until someone opens the lid,
there is no scientific measurement:
we don't know if the cat's alive or dead.
Now I'm no physicist, but I would think
that by the use of one's olfactory
senses — by following one's nose — the stink
would more than likely give the game away.
So, the Animal Liberation Front
will storm his lab and extricate poor Heidi
(I tipped them off), and after that I want
to dust his bench and make it nice and tidy.
In a parallel world, I'm certain that
there are more ways than one to skin a cat.

Epilogue

You sleep. It's like an accusation.
I watch the TV with the volume down
so's not to wake you. Your recrimination

resonates inside my buckled brain.
Tanita Tikaram discusses her career.
It's muggy with an outside chance of rain

this afternoon, the weathergirl with frosted hair
and too much blusher tells us. Siouxsie Sioux
turns solo in the graveyard shift of our affair.

And now some tips for tasty tapas. Cue
Jeremy with diet hints to combat stress,
It isn't what you eat, it's what eats you:

a dish of humble pie. How not to dress
for a sophisticated evening
at Madam Butterfly. How to impress

your escort, be vivacious, glittering,
and not cry when you hear the fat lass sing.

Josephine M. Fagan
El Sabor de Miel
(The Taste of Honey)

It looked like a black rock, a boulder, as broad as it was long. He couldn't quite focus it. The contours of the rock bent by hot air, made it look like it was moving, like a quivering horizon seen through petrol fumes evaporating from asphalt. That's how he remembered it, how he'd always describe it, when asked to recount this tale.

Consuelo Dulcia Mercedes Azucarada had inherited the largest cigarette factory in the region. Some said it was the largest in the country. Her father had built the place up from nothing. Every family in the surrounding area had a link with *La Compania Tabacalera de Azucarada.* Hunched shouldered, bent-backed workers, sweating like galley slaves peppered the hillsides owned by Señor Azucarada. Brown-handed farmers tended tobacco seedlings with a midwife's care. Whole generations gathered in each harvest. Carts ferried leaves to the factory to be transformed into their daily bread. Neat, pale fingers of señoritas and children grew stained with humid drudgery, fumbling over *papel de fumar*. Dextrous matrons were responsible for rolling their famous speciality, the Azucarada cigar. Bringing home a few more pesos than the other workers, they were the factory floor's élite until arthritis knotted their knuckles. Fathers toiled alongside sons until age bent them towards local tabernas. There they would sit drinking, old boys who had worked together all of their lives, played together as children and married each other's sisters. Wine fuelled pontification, opinions made by drawing on their experience of the world, (such as it was), and delivered whilst drawing on a cigarrillo, (an Azucarada cigarillo), until the cough killed them.

Señor Azucarada was *El Jefe of Colmena Grande*, but Señora Azucarada was the ambitious one, with all the bright ideas. She had a fertile mind and a body of surprising fecundity for one so small. La Señora bore six sons and a daughter Consuelo. All of her boys grew to be over six feet tall, towering over the workforce they would inherit on the death of El Jefe. Consuelo's fate was also predestined. She was taught to cook, clean and keep house, in readiness for her parents' dotage. Consuelo spent part of every day in the kitchen, where a large stone pot of honey was stored, along with other important items, on the top shelf. It was imported, expensive and kept especially for the boys. El Jefe did not think it decorous for ladies to smoke, however he firmly believed it appropriate to introduce his sons to the Azucarada cigar, as soon as they could hold one between their index and middle fingers without dropping it. It was far superior to the cigarillos the workers smoked, but it took some getting used to. Often the boys were sick after the strong tobacco. To take the taste away their mother doled out the honey like medicine, like a reward. After administering a sticky spoonful to one of her poor green sons, she'd replace the lid and hand the container to her daughter. Consuelo would put the heavy jar back on the top shelf. Often her fingers would find a dribble clinging to the side, or a frill of honey, squeezed out from under the lid, collaring the top of the pot. With the frisson of a secret drinker, Consuelo licked the remnants of every spillage. She was allowed a whole spoonful only at Christmas, and on her birthday. Slow to dissolve, she kept it on her mute, melting tongue as long as possible, like a beggar hiding a find of gold in his mouth. Eyes closed she savoured the generous, lingering, mesmerising taste, and the tongue-smack, tooth-coating afterglow. Wonderfully smooth yet crystalline, thick yet runny, its texture as complicated as its sweet, yellow smell. The essence of every flower plundered in its creation captured and sealed inside each precious crystal. It was the old gardener who first taught Consuelo about bees, hives and honey. Leaning on his spade, wiping the sweat from his eyes, he'd muse wistfully,

'Señorita, what I wouldn't give to be queen bee for one day...'

As she tended the garden with him, Consuelo imagined being able to disappear into the perfumed heart of a flower, and she began to envy the underbellies of insects.

When the revolution came, Señora Azucarada couldn't stop them. Her sons had inherited her fighting spirit, but their comfortable childhood gave them none of her survival instinct. One by one, the bruised bodies of her sons were buried in the church yard at Colmena Grande. Their daughter was little consolation, for the death of six fine young men. Maddened by his loss, El Jefe took his gun and his despair to the front line. Despite his age, tales of his reckless bravery were swapped by veterans in the Taberna de Colmena. Songs were written of his heroism. After the revolution, Saturday nights in the tavern were always marked by a toast to El Jefe, that he might rest in peace. Bit by bit, the survival instinct bled out of La Señora. She lasted one short year after the war was over, and was buried with her husband, next to their six long sons. After the funeral, her daughter ate the entire contents of the honey pot, alone in the garden.

Consuelo sent for Miguel Moscon, he had been her father's foreman, during war-time.

'I know little of the workings of the factory Miguel, I shall rely on you to run it the way El Jefe and La Señora would have wanted.'

But Moscon was an old man, too old to fight, and too old to oversee a business. Colmena Grande suffered. Tears and tales of hardship were brought to Consuelo. She found these deputations tiresome, so she wrote to a distant cousin, from the *not so grande* branch of the family, asking him to take over the running of the factory. From the day her cousin Pedro arrived, she delegated everything to him, refusing to see any more workers. The only visitors that ever came to La Casa Azucarada were Pedro and Padre Santo the priest. Moscon did not live long after he was sacked. Workers whispered that the loyal old foreman had died of shame.

Not entirely alone in the great house, Consuelo still had two servants. A maid, whom everyone called *'Abuela'*, because it seemed she had been born old. No one in Colmena Grande remembered a time when Abuela Boquilla had been young. She had always worked at the Casa Azucarada, and despite the nickname of 'grandmother', was the spinster of the parish. The second servant, a boy, whose name Consuelo could never remember, had been taken on to replace the old gardener. He helped with odd jobs and tended the flowers.

The house began to crumble, heat cleaved to the walls, peeling off the paint like a child's finger nails. Curtains rotted on their rods. Abuela's mind and sight were failing and her bones were growing old. She didn't notice, and Consuelo didn't care, that the hall needed sweeping, and the salons needed airing, and the mattresses needed shaking, and the silver needed polishing. Only two areas were immaculate, the kitchen and the flower garden, for Consuelo only had one passion in life, the taste of honey.

The first lot of bees she acquired were from Europe, a gentle Carniolan strain with moderate honey production, called Apis mellifera carnica. She began writing to the International Apiary Society, and through them, corresponded with some of the most eminent professors of entomology. Books on beekeeping lined the walls. Consuelo even made notes for the start of a book herself. It was to be a vast volume of recipes entitled *El Sabor de Miel*, designed for fellow devotees. It was so versatile, no matter what the recipe, Consuelo felt it could only be improved by a drizzle of honey. Her mouth could single out the taste, the same way some cooks fret about the salt.

When Padre Santo visited on the anniversary of El Jefe's death, she waxed the tips of her hair, sleeked her eyebrows and put on the dress she had not worn since the funeral. The table was polished like a mirror and the room illuminated with candles, all from her own bees' wax. They dined on honeyed chicken with caramelised onions, and glazed ham. Honey and water (her habitual drink), wine, hot toddies and her own potent brand of mead were brought to the table. The whole feast was splendid, but ah, the pudding! It was an amber monument to the bee.

'A recipe of my own invention.' She announced proudly, as old Abuela struggled in, bearing a sticky confection, in the shape of an enormous honeycomb. Padre Santo, full of compliments, talked politely of her hive, her garden and the weather, until emboldened by Consuelo's mead, the priest broached the subject of marriage.

'You are all alone here Señorita. One day the factory will need an heir, have you thought of taking a husband?'

'Padre, I cannot think of marrying so soon after my terrible loss.'

'Yes, just so, forgive me if I gave cause for offense Señorita.'

The truth is, we all have only so much passion in our souls. Some devote it all to a lover, some to their children, to an idea, or an ideal, others to a great cause. Consuelo's passion was entirely spent on her bees, because she loved the taste of honey. It was her balm, her medicine, her every meal. It was said she could not sleep at night without a spoonful of warm honey in her mouth. Her teeth rotted and she grew fat. Her tears and

El Sabor de Miel (The Taste of Honey)

her urine smelt of honey. The doctor warned her of the dangers of diabetes mellitus. Ignoring his advice, she preferred to take royal jelly, or her own propolis potions to keep her healthy. But she did reflect on what the priest had said in cold lonely moments, when her bees were out gathering pollen.

When the weather grew warmer, Señorita Azucarada would sit in her garden, watching the wagtail dance of her bees amidst blossoms and clover. Long into the evening she sat, watching them collecting nectar and pollen, the close, sticky air, thick with velvet hum. The whole stable block was given over to one enormous hive. At night, if she couldn't sleep, Consuelo would spread herself against the hot tingling walls of the old horse boxes feeling the vibrations, soothed by the rhythms of her workers and drones.

She had, for some time now, enjoyed a lively correspondence with one entomologist in particular, a certain Professor Gabriel Abejarron from *La Univerisad del Ciudad*. It was through him that she acquired her African Queen, a bee from Tanzania with a reputation for staggering honey production. He sent it by special courier, with a letter telling Consuelo of his proposed visit to her province in six months' time. He respectfully requested an audience with Consuelo, her new queen, and her colony of bees, suggesting they might enjoy a little honey tasting together. She replied, saying she would be delighted to meet Professor Abejarron at last, inviting him to stay for a week, or longer, if his schedule permitted.

The notepaper the professor used was pale yellow, a mixture of cream and gold. Consuelo often fancied it smelt of honey, as she kissed each one of the notes he had sent her, before locking them away in a lime-wood box, like love letters. Gabriel Abejarron, all velvet black hair and amber eyes, had swooped down on her through her bridal-veil mosquito net for years in her dreams. Mellifluous murmurings and nectar sweet kisses brushed her ear, like an insect's wings.

'Consuelo te adoro, mi vida!'

'Gabriel Abejarron te quiero...' she hummed, again and again, as the entomologist's passion swarmed over the honey plump flesh of her dreams. His was the only name that buzzed around in her head after Padre Santo had suggested she should marry. For more than a week after the African Queen arrived, Consuelo kept the creature in a special box in her bedroom. The box was hung from a silken cord over her bed. Each night Consuelo lay hot and naked beneath the buzzing pendant, in order to absorb the pheromones the queen bee secreted, that she might bewitch Abejarron.

Nine days later she killed the old queen bee by squashing her against the stable door, then replaced her with the new one. Consuelo smoked the agitated bees with fumes from her father's tobacco and they calmed, accepting their new African chief. Soon honey flowed. It would be ready for extraction just before the professor's visit. She and Abuela polished the house from top to bottom, bought new drapes and painted peeling walls. Then as the time drew near, they busied themselves in the kitchen, elbow deep in honey.

Pedro came to see Consuelo. He seemed agitated, he said the workers were restless at the factory. On and on he droned.

'Production has fallen, sales have fallen, wages are falling, the people are suffering, spirits are low and tempers are running high Señorita.'

Business at *La Compania Tabacalera de Azucarada* had been bad for some time. Consuelo's only passion was the taste of honey. She had no knowledge of, and no interest in the cigarette factory. The truth was, that behind this smoke screen of concern for the workers, Pedro's incompetence and greed had the place virtually bankrupt. His sticky fingers loved the taste of money. Ever since he came to Colmena Grande, he had been milking the profits.

'Señorita the workers are angry. I don't know how to calm them.'

'I don't want to hear about the factory. I put you in charge Pedro Azucarada. I pay you to deal with all of that. Now, be off! I am expecting a very important visitor, an eminent professor. Do not distract me with tales of ungrateful workers.'

'But what shall I say to them Señorita?'

'I don't care. Say what you like.'

Pedro had not known of anyone, apart from himself and the priest, visit Consuelo since her mother died. He suspected she was inventing excuses.

Back in the cigarette factory, the workers demanded to know what Señorita Azucarada had said about the crisis. Diverting their anger away from himself, Pedro told them exactly what she had said. Agitation ripened to revolution.

'She doesn't care about the workers.'

'It's not the same since the old man died.'

'She treats that grand house like her castle.'

'Si! She never comes down to Colmena Grande like El Jefe used to.'

'She doesn't know how we live.'

'She does not see how hard life is these days, especially for the widows and the orphans.'

'Nothing has changed since the war. Is this what we fought for?'

'*Hermanos* unite!'

'*Adelante! Vamanos a La Casa Azucarada!*'

Consuelo had taken to visiting the hive without wearing her long white gown and veiled hat — seeing no need these days. She felt closer to her bees, than to any man alive. She slipped out to the stable block for one last look at her new queen's colony before the professor's arrival. Inside the house, Abuela smoothed her hair and her apron the moment she heard the knocking. The old maid had a speech of welcome all prepared, but it was not Abejarron who had hammered at the front door. Opening it she stood face to face with a mob. For a silent, split second, pair after pair of angry black eyes, each menacing as a smoking rifle barrel, fixed on Abuela. Then a cry flew up propelled by a clenched fist baying for revolution, splitting the silence that had hung like a veil over the crowd. Workers pushed past her, knocking Abuela to the ground.

As the mob were setting off up the hill to Consuelo's house, no one had noticed the car pull up in the village square. A large black car, with a gold stripe down the side and the tall, dark stranger with velvet black hair and amber eyes, getting out.

'Where is she?' demanded the crowd.

'Who?'

'Who do you think? Her royal highness *La Regina de Colmena!*'

Workers swarmed through the house to the sala grande.

'Look at all this rich food.'

Tobacco-stained hands plunged into the honey feast prepared especially for Professor Abejarron.

'There are enough candles here to light a cathedral.'

Fistfuls of them were snatched up, and stuffed into threadbare pockets, along with silver candelabra. Dirty children who had tagged along behind the mob, began to demolish a vast pudding in the shape of a honeycomb. It had pride of place in the centre of the waxed wooden table which had shone like a mirror only moments before, and which now was obscured by debris and desperate hands.

No one noticed the tall dark stranger with black velvet hair and amber eyes, walking up the hill behind them. Gabriel approached the house hearing the hum of the rabble through the open door. To the side of the house he saw a splendid flower garden, and behind it a stable block. Screwing up his eyes, Professor Abejarron saw a swarm of jet button bees around what looked like a large black rock, a boulder, as broad as it was long, on the ground in front of the stables. The whole scene seemed to sway in the heat. He was intrigued, all of these flowers to collect pollen from, and they were congregating around a rock. Gabriel wasn't afraid of the insects, he had been stung many times in the course of his work. As he drew nearer, the sound of furious humming crescendoed. He lit a cigar to calm the angry bees, and some of the insects started to lift. Then he took off his jacket, put it over his head like a bridal-veil, and rolled down his shirt sleeves. Gabriel neared and peered at the boulder. The black swarm lifted. What he had taken to be a rock was the purple, swollen body of a woman, curled up into a ball, lying quite still. Porcupine-peppered, barbed by more than a hundred venomous stings, her fat body was bloated beyond all recognition. A sticky yellow liquid, like honey, oozed from her wounds.

Ever after that day, the day of the factory workers' riot, the names of Señorita Consuelo Dulcia Mercedes Azucarada and Professor Gabriel Abejarron were linked together, married by history. Hers was the first of several cases described in the literature, by the now famous entomologist, concerning a strain of so-called 'killer bees' in the Americas. Bees that had been brought over from Africa to increase honey production, to satisfy those who love the taste.

Marlynn Rosario

Always The Indian

Your braids he explained, *your skin, my pale face*.
He skipping-roped her to the bombsite tree.
Squint-eyed he pointed his finger-gun,
galloped off with the tin star, fringes flying.
Obediently she waited, tasting his dust.
She knew the Saturday movie rules.
The papoosed baby dug plastic fingers
through her dress, bark scraped her scalp.

Always the Indian, she learned to hop,
to sing with a finger in her mouth,
to offer hands and feet for binding.
Tex, Roy, Matt, his names were shiny, silver bullets.

He called her *Little Rock*, she was Rock.
He called her *Whispering Breeze*, she was Raging.
He called her *Still Water*, she was Running.

Raging stamped and struggled, loosened knots.
Rock pulled the baby from her back.
Running rode the splintered stick,
winged her hair with feathers,
streaked her face with brilliance.
She bowed a branch with singing string,
gathered stones and sharpened.
Waited his coming, that dust in the distance.

Missing

The scent of *Impulse* overpowered bread and new cloth.
In my hands broken threads; beneath a shaking ceiling
I stitched to the throb of *Ultimate Kaos* and *Crush*.

She left, mouth sour with defiance,
slamming polyfilla from cracks;
the door smack a heavy hand across my face.
I banged on the window, screaming,
but she was gone, the holes of her tracking heels
already closing with the falling sleet.

I'd forgotten the needle in my fist,
blood smeared the pane;
that is how it was.

Of course I've warned her, but not this time.
Towerblocks behind dwarf our street.
People shout from blinded windows,
things fall from balconies, we're on the edge.
I've told her, keep your head down, walk near the wall.
The park in front is full of rumours.
I've told her to avoid it, but not this time.

Worry folds a line from nose through cheek,
corrugates my forehead, fans my hair with silver.
Worry and time.
She dyes her hair and talks of piercing.

I wait and watch, as though looking will bring her back.
My reflection slips in the double-glazing, trapped.
Snow has emptied the street, the glass tells me nothing.

Headlights rock the house —
darkness, light, darkness.

I want her back.
I want to tell her, this is how it is
broken threads, suddenly a door slams,
fine lines appear, craziness.

Travelling By Numbers

Poppies felt-tip the verges
keeping our East we go South,
a tractor curries the field.

This morning her emptied room,
her screams, that old fear of flying things.
I caught the creature in drained glass,
trapped it with careful card,
left it to freedom on the open sill.

Now, weighted by her nineteen years,
jigsawed by possessions, blind at the rear,
we snail the motorway umbilical.

Looking back she is all my view.
She nods in the mirror frame,
beats time to something I cannot hear,
looks past my sly eyes to something I cannot see.
I bite my tongue on remembering.

Arriving is goodbye, I leave her
a moth bewildered after brief entrapment.
Keeping our East, returning is already familiar.
She is South of the North of me.

Sue Vickerman
The Exorcism

Susheela Mataji the holy woman has arrived in the village; I can hear the drumbeat. Feel it. I take the short cut home from school. Thud, thud; a vibration in the warm air. Across the onion fields, thud, thud; the slap of my sandals keeping time.

The drum belongs to Mataji's companion, her high-voiced eunuch. Looks like a man from behind but there's something in his face. Cooks and keeps house for Mataji while she does her pujas, wedding spells, exorcisms, funeral singing; the things she's hired for.

Home from school I step out of my sandals in the deep shadow of the awning in front of our dwelling. School gets kicked into a corner. Home is barefoot. I sluice my head under a cup of water drawn from the pot by the door. The water slips from my oiled head over my forehead and nose, and snakes away across the caked earth, picking up dust. I drink the remaining half-cup and fling the aluminium tumbler back in the pot. From inside the black doorway my mother shrieks - you'll break that pot, and then what? But I'm already away down the track, the sun on me like a laser beam. I'm zinging like an electric guitar, like my uncle's sitar that whined intensely all on its own when he left it outside.

I'm not her son. I'm not Mr Nambudiri's pupil. I'm a working guy, going to my job. And I'm in love.

I walk backwards to slow down. I slick my hair forward with my palms, flick the front strands back, then rub off the coconut oil down my shirt front. The village shimmers in the distance across the deserted plain. The plain looks flat and smooth, but it is deeply rutted earth, too painful to cut across without sandals. No other dwellings have been built at this side of the onion fields, apart from my father's sister's shack away towards the hills, and the ashram that I am heading for now.

The ashram is the home of another holy woman, of a different kind; not like Susheela Mataji who comes from the next village and is my mother's mother's cousin. Sister Ananda came to our village from Europe before I was born. She has always attracted important visitors: rich people; Brahmins from Pune; white foreigners. They arrive in the market, looking for guides to show them the way. My cousin has been able to set up a rickshaw firm to carry these city visitors from the bus in the market to her ashram. People like that are not the sort to struggle over the onion fields in the heat of the day, like everyone else.

Like Susheela Mataji, Sister Ananda doesn't do women's work. When there are several ashram guests, my mother is employed to do the food. The pay is better than any work in the village. Meanwhile, Sister Ananda will be busy teaching the visitors to chant and do pujas. They buy coloured powders from the market and carefully draw mandalas on the threshold, copying from a book held in one hand. They pick flowers in Sister Ananda's garden and make designs from the petals on the floor of the prayer hall.

But Ananda, being a foreigner, can't help people in the traditional ways. Not like Susheela Mataji.

I'm still panting, moving too fast in the late afternoon sun. Suddenly everything's glowing: the fields of cracked mud which stretch to the horizon, golden as turmeric; the whitewashed walls of the ashram, honeyed as a baby's skin.

Our dwelling in the distance is a frog squatting in the mud. The tiny shape moving like a cockroach on the ground in front of the hut is my mother. I know that she's rolling chappatis. A scrawny, nagging female with flying hands which slap my younger siblings. I shrug her off, turn around, face my work-place. Hot ripples begin dissolving my insides like illegal liquor.

The verandah of the ashram is cool, clean-swept. My feet enjoy the novelty of smooth tiles, recognising a world I played in when I was very small, when my mother was taken on to sweep up and keep the scorpions out while Sister Ananda was away on pilgrimages.

Since the last black moon, I've been employed here. When Sister Ananda noticed that I'm now taller than my mother, and muscular, she took me on to fetch water from Mali's well each day after school. For each bucket I get a coin. Three buckets every evening until the rainy season, when the ashram's own well will fill up again. It is my job to cross this cool threshold every day, where my feet are soothed by the smoothness, unlike the crust of compacted earth on which I eat, sleep, do homework for Nambudiri, and argue with my kid brothers and sisters.

I've been in love since yesterday, when Sister Ananda sent me with the third and last bucket into the bathroom of a dormitory on the first floor. The foreigner slipped out past me quickly as I, sweating, walked in, the red plastic on my head making me really tall.

Yellow hair! Thin wisps like grass on the sannyasini's forehead. In the manner of foreigners, she's looking at my face, not away, but she's smiling in the closed-mouth way of local women. Her sari is ochre, like the Western Rajneeshi followers I saw in Pune once. It's pulled tightly under her arm and trails limply over her shoulder, unstarched, and as she turns sideways very close to me, edging past in the doorway, the flesh of her waist gets exposed beneath the wafting cloth; a flash of white, like a fish darting away. Moon-white. How can anyone living on this planet have a body so white? What about the effects of the sun, that turns everything else in the world golden?

When she slips away I smell her: not the spicy warmth of flesh but a scent as cool as eucalyptus, yet sharp, like a squeezed lime.

After she'd gone I let the bucket down from my head and carried it into the bathroom through the low doorway. Clustered in the corner were three plastic bottles: all kinds of shampoo for her yellow hair. I unscrewed each top, sniffing. Each of the scents was part of her smell, but not all of her. Her blue eyes had looked into my face as though she wanted to know me. I wanted to snatch that slippery fish; to know whether her whole body was so startlingly white. She'd be cool to the touch, like inside an icebox. Me warm, her cool; her skin blue-white, like the moon.

The Exorcism

Today I take the first bucket to the kitchen. No sign of anyone. The second bucket — Ananda's bathroom on the ground floor. I hear a lone voice chanting in the prayer hall. I adjust my dhoti. The third bucket is still on my head when Sister Ananda meets me coming over the verandah and asks me whether I can return after dark and be her guide across the fields to where the exorcism will take place. Sister Ananda has lived here until her face is dark and wizened as a nut. Her frail body wrapped in white cloth is as bent as my great-grandmother's. She indicates that I should set down the third bucket there on the verandah.

'Tomorrow only two buckets, Kumar,' she says in Marathi.

Gone. Yesterday's visitors have gone. First I'm crushed, let down, then within a second I'm stiff, drawing a sharp breath: here's the yellow-haired foreigner approaching Sister Ananda from the doorway. Again, the smile like yesterday; the eyes, the loose swing of her arms like bleached ropes.

I offer to take the third bucket to the first floor bathroom but Sister Ananda says something to her remaining visitor, who moves to take it by the handle. I step forward quickly and try to take it from her.

'It's heavy,' I say in Marathi. The girl pulls as though to take it from my grip. Her hand is blue-veined, somehow unused.

'It's not work for foreigners,' I say. She won't understand.

'They don't know how to carry things on their head,' I say to Sister Ananda, who only smiles as the girl keeps on reaching. The girl's pale straw hair brushes my shoulder. Ananda just walks away as we begin carrying the bucket together. In such ways as this, Sister Ananda will always be foreign.

This wild dream flashes through my brain, where I reach out ...

We just walk, unevenly, through the interior room, slopping water, gripping hard. I'm breathing in as much as I can of her smell. Wisps from her bowed head tickle my face. I see that her sari is slipping from her shoulder altogether; we have to stop on the staircase so that she can hoist it.

'It doesn't suit your skin,' I say. She laughs a little, pushing the loose end of her sari into the fold at the waist in an unusual way. By doing this, she reveals the choli fitted tightly over her breasts. She shouldn't.

We continue lifting, slopping, brushing hips very lightly at the turn into the dormitory, then she lets me place the bucket inside the doorway of the narrow bathroom partitioned off in one corner. I duck out of the bathroom again and see her, further in the room, perched on one of the low wooden platforms on which the visitors sleep. Her cheeks have turned pink like those of someone from the north. She says something I don't understand, smiling. I take a step towards her, wondering whether that's the right thing. She is suddenly flustered, ushering me away with her hands, frowning, upset. I step back from the great gulf that yawns between me and people like her. We're on different planets.

I hurry out of the ashram feeling soaked, a monsoon-drenching. I need to shake myself, like a dog emerging from the river. I slouch along the track approaching our ugly home and the scolding from my mother for forgetting to stop by the flour mill with our order. But when I arrive, my mother only shouts at me from inside,

'Feed your brothers and sisters quickly, then lay them down. We'll have to set off in no time at all.'

I have never slept on anything other than a straw mat in my entire life, my brothers and sisters wriggling under our shared blanket. Hot, sticky, baby skin. Across the fields is a cool, white snake, coiled on her wooden bed. The gulf between us is as wide as the ravine that cuts through our mountains to the west of the village.

I'm furious with my siblings for being slow and fractious. Slap, slap.

My father's sister's husband is to be exorcised of the demon that causes him to drink then beat his wife and daughters. My father's sister went to Sister Ananda for help first, asking for employment for her husband, in order that he would be occupied and kept away from his friends. Sister Ananda didn't offer him any work, but she treated the wounded face of my father's sister with her medicines.

Being a foreigner, Ananda hasn't got power over the men. Only Susheela Mataji has the power to exorcise the demons out of the men who drink themselves into a stupor every day under the banyan tree in the market.

In the end my father's sister sent for Mataji to come for full moon, although Mataji's fees are high.

The moon is massive in the sky but I carry a lamp to give myself more of a role, leading Sister Ananda and her girl — away from their gateway towards the distant drumbeat. I walk only a little ahead, hearing their breathing, knowing that she is immediately behind me from her scent. She stumbles between the hardened clods in flimsy, foreign-made sandals, while Sister Ananda's glide is silent. The moon hovers. Our blue shadows tumble across the rutted fields. The drum is in the earth, a tremor coming from deep down. I imagine the moonlight to be refreshing, yet find a trickle of sweat running down my face. I want to look back, see how her skin reflects the glow of the moon like a still pool. I suddenly need water, the cool feel of it pouring over me. The night is deceptively hot.

Small lights are wavering across the fields like fireflies, converging from many directions. They seem to bob in time with the drumbeat, everyone in unison. Beyond the dark silhouette of some parched bushes, the bright frontage of my relative's dwelling appears, decorated for the occasion with very many small oil lamps. A freshly woven awning has been slung over the square of earth reserved for dignitaries in front of the shack.

When I slow up a little, a hand brushing against my buttock shocks me like a sting. Sister Ananda and her girl — they seem to be clustering to me. I step back, confused. Were they reaching for my lamp? The girl's eyes, they're running all over me. I really think so. I don't look up to check; I just want to feel it.

The hostess, another of my relatives, is suddenly between us. I am pushed in the direction of the village youths, while the two honoured guests are led into the bright square of light to be seated on freshly-laid matting. But we are all seated within the circle of the drum. Its vibration ripples out among us like when a stone hits a pond.

My father's sister is ugly and argumentative. Tonight I notice how very black-skinned she is. A hard life of picking onions. My father's sister's eight daughters are as ugly and argumentative as she is. I look down at my hands, my bare legs, as though seeing my own skin tone for the first time; a family likeness to my cousins that I can't escape. In this moment I get a fizzing passion for moon-white skin, such as I've never felt before.

My heart is thumping in time to the throb, throb of taut skin struck by a flat hand. Across the heads of a hundred squatting villagers I find myself staring at the girl, her face like the moon among a dark blur of special guests who are being served tea and sweetmeats. I know I'm nothing to her, hidden in shadow. I can still feel the touch of her hand. I want it to have been her hand.

Susheela Mataji has been making preparations at the dwelling for hours.

As her strange, high-voiced partner beats on and on, parading in a slow circle, crying out occasionally, Mataji is wordlessly putting the finishing touches to her shrine in the centre of the square of earth below the awning. She has concocted it out of leaves, flowers, stones, and tall ears of crops saved and dried from last year's harvest. I'm squashed into a small area with my classmates. Rab whispers,

'All it needs now is a string of onions dangling in the middle!' We all fall against each other laughing.

Mataji is using coloured powders to draw a mandala on the ground. I fixate on Sister Ananda's girl. I realise that she is making notes, and that she and Ananda murmur to each other sometimes. Maybe she's married, in her own country. Offerings of fruit are now being placed before the shrine by various devout villagers. Throb, throb, throb, in the ground beneath us. We are being vibrated, rattled into silence. We increase our concentration, become motionless, squatting on the ground under the giant moon.

Now Susheela Mataji stands before the crowd and starts ranting the many names of the *devi* in Marathi and other languages. My neighbour says too loudly that she's doing it to show how far she's travelled, but it only adds up to a few villages. I agree she sounds rather foolish, considering that Sister Ananda sitting right behind her has seen the whole world. Sister Ananda looks very intent. The girl's face is reflecting the light of the moon. Then the girl suddenly wipes a hand over her forehead and trawls her fingers back across her hair, and I'm dazzled. It must be the pounding silence, the heat, the heady sandalwood: I 'm paralysed and gasping for air. No — it's *her power over me*.

She's a goddess.

The three drunks who are said to be demon-possessed have been sent forward out of the crowd. The suffering relatives are giving accounts of the demons that have taken over their men. I give my head a shake, trying to get a grip. Nudging, I whisper to my huddled group that I'd drink under the banyan tree too if I were the husband of my father's sister.

After descriptions of their evil behaviour, the drum beat quickens. Blue eyes, moon face. Eyes that are precious stones among the dark, bowed heads. Jewels launching spears of moonlight as she glances all around. Is she searching for me? I believe I can see her shoulders and chest moving up and down, as though she's panting, as I am, in the crushing heat. I start to breathe in unison with her, staring hard enough for her to feel my eyes, so that she's bound to pick me out.

Susheela Mataji begins a continuous rant addressed to the possessed men, weaving and circling between them, whispering then shouting in each of their ears, faster then slower then faster until even I start to feel strange, dizzy; meanwhile her partner circles the cowering threesome with his own squealing-pig chant, pounding the taut membrane until I feel it reverberating on the skin stretched over my forehead. Round and round he circles; pounding, pounding, until people start to relieve their feelings by crying out more accusations. Sister Ananda looks rather dazed, sipping one of the cups of tea being handed around regularly among the special guests. I feel my blood bubbling up like from a goat's spasming carcass. I'm hooked, being pulled into the girl's visible, increasing agitation. I taste the tea when she sips and then gasps, pouring the whole cup into the ground. I hold my breath; I feel like water ebbing into sand. Her jewel-eyes have never stopped flickering all around, picking up faces in the crowd then dropping them. In the heat, the oppressive moonlight, the press of the crowd, I find myself on the verge of screaming out along with the others.

In the moment when my shout reaches the well-lit square where the frenzied men are quaking and shaking, I am picked up and held; plucked by her eyes, lifted out of the crowd. I'm levitating, clasping my knees in hands like claws, suspended in mid-air on shards of her cut-diamond eyes. I've stopped breathing altogether; feel myself swirling and drowning. Her mouth is wide open, too. Like two fish, we're gulping for air.

Later, I don't know which of us it was who cried out; whether it was even both of us.

In the same instant, the three men fall one by one to their knees in a frenzy, shivering and trembling, writhing and frothing with staring eyes. Susheela Mataji crouches down to be level with their ears, each in turn, her words reduced now to a whisper. She stops the drum with an irritated flapping of her hand. The men go quiet and still, lying peacefully, looking, in fact, the same as they always look in the late afternoon under the banyan tree. Susheela Mataji stands up at the front of the awning and addresses the silent crowd to say the demons are gone.

'Peace'. She uses the Sanskrit word. Everyone's exhausted. Peace.

Dark figures start to melt back into the fields, their lamps receding into the night. I make through the subdued villagers and reach the two who I must lead to the ashram. The girl's eyes are lowered, and I see blue shadows below them on her milk face. It's the first time I've though of milk. Moon, milk, slippery fish, white snake. Blue veins; hands that have never been used.

Sister Ananda tells me that I'm looking at her guest. She doesn't say 'too much'. She doesn't scold. Everyone's milling around, saying goodnight. The girl now raises her face, slowly, keeping her eyes averted, and passes me the lamp, moving close until the lamp touches my dhoti. Thigh brushing thigh. Then she moves away. I grasp the lamp, wishing to catch her silver fish hand. I take in some of the damp breath that has just left her lips. Then, when Sister Ananda pats her girl lightly on the hip to signal that we should start for home, this one blue-veined hand reaches like a minnow flickering through water, touching my own hip to pass on the instruction:

'Come.'

Sunrise. I'm pushing the buffalo out of her stall, beating her leather arse with a stick, chivvying her slow hulk onto the track. This is the precious, cool time of day. It will disappear too soon. The slight chill in the air normally makes me alert, but this morning I need to fling my arm over our buffalo's back, rough as tree bark, and let myself be half-carried to the river.

As the buffalo wades in, setting the mud of the river bed swirling, I have the urge to plunge after her, immerse myself until my blood is chilled in my veins, until the warm smell of my own skin has turned into the scent of water.

An hour later, when everyone has left for the fields and I'm about to leave for school, I spot Sister Ananda. She's picking her way across the onion fields in front of our house, carrying a leather satchel.

'Business in Pune,' she calls, waving the bag at me.

'I'll be back on the last train. I'd like you to carry in two buckets all the same,' she adds. 'I'll look forward to a bath when I return.'

In a second I'm kicking my sandals off again, taking the lid from the pot by the door and reaching in for the tin cup, trembling. I drink two cups so fast that I hardly swallow. My tipped up mouth overflows, water coursing down my chin, running into the top of my shirt. Nambudiri won't lay eyes on me today. Maybe never again. I fling my school shirt into a corner along with my dhoti, grab my denim jeans and pull them on, and set off in my sweat-drenched vest. Looking down at it I see dark circles of my own belly through the several large holes. I know who I am.

When I cross the threshold of the ashram with the red bucket on my head, hours too early, it's silent. I feel calm. I'm a guy with a job; a golden boy who carries water for a wage. I'm tall and strong, born and raised in a hard, cracked-open landscape.

I move confidently through the ground floor rooms, the red bucket still on my head. Up the stairs to the dormitory, so quietly that a tiny lizard adjusting its position on the ceiling catches my ear.

From the doorway I can see that she's lying on her stomach on the wooden bed, her chin propped on one hand while the other is tapping fairly absently at the keyboard of a whirring lap-top computer. Her sari is thrown over a piece of washing line strung between the window grilles. She's lying there in her underclothing, the tight choli revealing the precise shape of her breasts and shoulders. The long underskirt is drawn in with a string above her hips, leaving an expanse of snaking, translucent flesh where her waist curves in and out like an eel, as though there were no hard bone-matter in her body. So wasteful; just throwing away something so good, this snaking shape: elegant, precious. I can't understand why she doesn't hide it from everyone in the world, revealing herself only as an intimate gift.

I call 'water' in my language as I move through the doorway into the dormitory. She's aware of me looking. She must know something of who I am; what I dream of. She speaks without looking over, flicks off the power, closes the lid and neatly lifts the lap-top from the bed to the floor. Then she gets up, moves towards me, reaches up for the bucket. Cool lime flesh.

I turn away, dealing with the bucket myself, ducking it from my head and into the bathroom cubicle.

When I come back out she's just standing there. I move past her and walk to her bed in the middle of the room. The shutters are pulled half-closed, filtering the morning sun. Saffron light slants across the concrete floor. I think of my father, when we're all sprawled on our bedmats, after the final lamp is put out; when the small ones are long since asleep and I am drifting into oblivion. My father, thumping the platform on which he sleeps with my mother. My mother, outlined in the moonlight, sidling over from the earth-oven that she's been banking up for the night with a flat plate of dung. My father banging again with the flat of his hand, not as a request but to signal his need.

I sit on the edge of her low bed and bang on the centre of it with the flat of my hand. I present the bed to her, running my hand across the whole of its area. She doesn't move, just looks at her bed. Perhaps she doesn't know this gesture. So I begin pounding, rhythmic, like the drumbeat, watching her mysterious face.

In time with my rhythm she takes a few barefoot steps: pad, pad. Now she is beside me, her waist at a level for my face to press into it. I pull my dirty, holed vest over my head in one movement and fling it somewhere. Here is my moist, golden skin, smelling of spices and buffalo.

In return, she unbuttons, unties, steps out of her clothing and holds out her hands, smiling a modest smile of closed lips. A slippery fish, I catch her in a flash. Brilliant as rippling water, the tang of lime, and so white — oh, so white.

Karen Laws

Pompeii

Warm streets of woven hessian.
Buildings baked
in dusty spices
paprika deep.
Fireplaces
in burnt Egyptian gold,
carbon cold in the grate.

Cracked light
glowing on mosaics
dusty peach in
breathless heat,
ruddy flesh ablaze
on brothel walls,
tangles of arms, legs,
falling saffron silks,
tops notched on cinnamon beds
from endless shoes,
countless men.

Dazzling orange trees,
bees lazing on honeysuckle
then a garden
of terracotta corpses
mouths wide at sandsharp air
backs bent
at iron firedrops,
twisted from burning.

The naked earth now hushed,
still,
softly blushing pomegranate.

Kriss Nichol

Hyacinth Days

Sprouting bulbs on a windowsill
crack
and in that moment a trapdoor opens.
Passing through I enter
familiarity
and breathe in sensory
triggers;
ink, pencil shavings, chalkdust, cabbage.
I see the hands on heads,
the child in the corner,
knuckles rapped with a ruler.
I hear playground noises
intermingled with name calling
and the sound of latches
on outside toilets.
Milk bottles rattle in crates
as they are moved
from beside the radiator,
their lukewarm contents
soon to be guzzled
with distaste.
A gentle breeze fans
my face
as delicate as trailing
daddy-long-legs legs,
brushing away cobwebs
of disappointment.
Alchemy has taken
place here
in the foundry of daydreams
and perfumed air.

Brighid Morrigan
Louise

Louise's life was punctuated by eggs. Egg collection. Egg delivery. Eggs for breakfast, eggs for tea. Eggs with soldiers. Louise marched to the hens like a soldier. She stamped to attention by the gate and put the feed bucket down. She shouted orders to herself to unhook the gate to the hen orchard. She stamped attention on the other side. Saluted. Left, right, left, right. Attention. She unbolted the hen shed door. All the hens scurried around her feet. They were not orderly. They pecked the grass, the trees, the sky. They raced around the water trough. They mumbled and gossiped. Louise filled the food hopper with her bucket of swept-up grain and flung the kitchen leftovers across the dried earth.

'Egg soldiers,' she shouted. An older hen bullied two younger pullets. They fluttered and flapped.

'Quiet,' she shouted, but they paid no attention.

'I've come for your eggs.'

Inside the shed it was warm. It smelt warm. Powdery and fleshy. Hen flesh. Hen feet. Hen shit. It smelt of gossip. Hen murmurs, hen whispers. Challenges and stand downs. Back ups and back offs. Louise collected the eggs into her empty feed bucket. They clattered around inside the rim. Pale eggs, wrinkled eggs, eggs ragged with bumps of extra crust. Thin shells, dark shells, blotched shells. Cool eggs, warm eggs, almost hot eggs.

Inside the shed one hen sat tight. Distracted. Vicious. Upset at the interruption. There was nothing to do but wait. She sat on a hen box opposite and watched. The hen concentrated. Blanked out the world. Went somewhere. Went blind. Turned deaf. It was nearly ready. It sat tight, glued to the nest. It watched the wall. Stared at the grain in the wood. White and mottled. It stared at the cobwebs. Falling down cobwebs. It waited. Louise waited. The feathers on its back were rhythmically patterned. She searched her fingers for scabs to pick. Her knuckles, her nails. And her wrists. She looked for any kind of scrape; a kitten scratch, a nail scar, a nail bite. Flea bite scabs. Itchy scalp scabs. Dirt under her finger nails. Splinters from her crusted eyes. Dog hairs on her jumper. Straw knitted into the wool. Then it happened. The temperature rose. The sun shifted. The shed almost rocked on its mud foundations. The hen stood exposing its flaking legs. If it could, it would grunt. If it could, it would go to the seaside. To the moon. Drawn to its full height it hovered. Silent. It had all of Louise's attention. She froze, vigilant not to make even the smallest sound. The shed turned quiet. It was an intense wait. An imminent wait. A weighty wait. Then it happened. The egg dropped to the nest. Laid. Hot. Hullabaloo erupted. The hen dashed about headless and frantic like church bells after midnight mass. Children after the school bell.

'Happy the bloody egg's out,' it croaked. 'Happy. Happy. Get on with the day. I've done it. I've done it again. Where are the others. I need a drink.' Louise let it out of the shed and held the freshest egg. A brand new egg. She didn't feel much like marching back. She stood and held the hot egg in both hands, wrapped in her fingers. The world.

Janine Langley McCann
A cake fit for a skin-bird

I've a friend on Marsh Avenue, the one that sweeps over the brow of the valley in a perfect arc, with big detached houses and sports fields opposite. I've played 'kerplunk' with them once, Jacqueline and her brother, in his bedroom. I must have snuck in then, because, this time when I go round, I never get past the kitchen door. I've been traipsing the streets all night in the gear; the Docs, the braces, waiting for someone to see. It's taken six weeks' paper round and all my bank money but I've got the Crombie now. The Crombie's everything.

'Taste some,' Jackie says to me; cupping her hand under a bit she's just cut off. Her and her Mum have made a big cake thing with crispies in. Strings of caramely stuff trail off it like sweet spit.

'What's in it?' I go, acting rock-hard, not looking keen, but I'd gladly shag smelly Bob Gibbins for a bit.

Then Jackie — giggling like an idiot — only starts scoffing the bit she's just offered me. I go beetroot. Her Mum smiles at me. She doesn't look tired or old like my Mum. She looks like she's just had her cheeks buffed up with Mr. Sheen does Jackie's Mum.

'Go on, try a little piece,' she says, and cuts me off some more.

'What's in it?' I go again. But I don't hang about this time. I sneak my bubbly into the snot-rag in my pocket and bite in. And I stand at the door, all awkward like, just rolling it around in my mouth, tears welling up in my eyes and ask myself how this can be done, while Jackie — perfect she is —

reels off the ingredients with her Mum nodding away beside her:

'Three quarters of a pound of rice crispies. One quarter of a pound of toffees. A tablespoon of golden syrup. One quarter of a pound of butter...'

Nothing will ever taste the same.

When I walk in our door our Nidge thumps my head sideways, says, 'Skin-bird eh? Haa.' Acting like the eldest, him, since our Robert's joined up.

The kitchen windows are blind with steam from the big tin pan and the braising steak in it smells like dog meat. I drape myself around the doorpost, still chewing the last bit of crispie cake that I tried like fuck to save so Mum could try it. So she'd know.

I say, 'Can we do this recipe Mum? Jackie Ashdene told me. It's gorgeous, really gorgeous. It's three quarters of rice crispies, a quarter of toffees... A quarter of butter...'

My Mum, sharp-eyed, clocks me sideways, goes, 'No you bloody-well can't.'

Jo Morris
Silent Running
from a novel in progress

M
Am I the only one who loves old women's skin? It calls to me. It is comforting. My Nanna — and yes I call her Nanna, I will not wrap her up in the taught shroud of Grandmother — has skin which is warm with wrinkles. Soft as tissue paper. Mottled brown as moth wings, and as fine. A long time ago, in that other wave of life, I climbed a Greek hill with her, and we came into a village. Black-skirted women approached us. They stopped and stroked my face. They liked my skin. Their brown grooved faces were cool like snakes. Three — or maybe even four — generations of skin in the shadow of a Greek doorway, and they were celebrating mine. Theirs was better. Even so. It was hard to read their faces, despite the sketching of their skin.

My face has changed since, at least it feels as though it has. No mirrors. The paint around the doorframe is the colour of the dust on the Greek road, dirt orange, but the walls are not quite true to the green which nibbled at its edges. Is it the wall that is glossy cool, or is it my cheek, my chin, my tongue? The paint is sour and tastes of dust.

Shona
I found the woman in the graveyard at about half-past-three. She was just a dark shape stooped over a grave shaped like a shallow bath full of green glass pebbles. I had been sitting on the steps, enjoying the cool air in my

nostrils, waiting for Melanie to return with my keys. I was looking across the space at a large statue of Mary with her arms outstretched in a *'why me?'* position, and wondering at the vivid turquoise of her dress, when I saw her. She was so very still, that for a moment or two I was unsure and thought, *what is it?* When she did move, I thought of large deer and other wandering mammals; then felt my spine slip with a chill and was scared for a second by other possibilities. Stupid, stupid. I saw her heave herself upright and became immediately brave.

'Can I help you?'

There was no response from the shape. I moved forwards, picking my way past polished black and gold stones carefully, until I was standing close enough to it to be certain that it was a fairly elderly woman. The woman's fingers traced the worn words on an older, mottled green stone. *Claire Rothbury, Beloved,* and dates. The grave was one of the smallest ones, a child's. I felt slightly strange, not really here, and had to swallow hard on acid which rose in my throat saying, *where's Hugo? This is his job*. I bit it in and in the meantime the woman's movements slowed, and I felt relieved at realising it was just a split-second. *This is me and I'm coping*, I thought, so I said a little too loudly —

'Are you looking for someone you knew? I mean any *particular* grave?' As the woman straightened and looked at me I felt my face scorching. I'm not used to talking to strangers, that's Hugo's speciality, his job in fact; and although it would make life a lot easier if I could keep a cool face, I still find it difficult. So, to hide it I dusted my hands on my skirt and instead of staring at the woman, glanced down at the grave.

'Was this your child?'

The woman shrugged fat shoulders under a too-small dufflecoat. *Why on earth did I ask that?* The shrug was so weak it seemed at odds with her bulk. Perhaps it *was* hers. No, that would be impossible, given the dates on the stone. But there was something in that shrug which made me wonder. The spit rose again, but I focused hard on her hairy brown coat which was tight under her armpits. A small looped ribbon was pinned to one lapel, and I couldn't help but notice the *Cancer Research* tag hanging from its hem and fluttering madly in the slight breeze.

'Would you like a cup of tea?'

I don't know what prompted me to ask, but there, it was said. I wasn't sure how Hugo would react, I never can tell really, what it is he thinks, which is part of his appeal, I suppose. But Hugo was otherwise engaged, and the lady was outside with me; so I thought *what the hell* — two non-Hugo words in one day — *I can do this*. I flapped at my skirt while I waited for an answer, but when she didn't give one I asked her again. She didn't seem to understand what I was saying, and when I looked at her properly and saw her worn tanned skin and thick black hair, I realised that she might be foreign. So, slightly surprised, I mimed the offer to the woman, who nodded. I pointed towards the church and smiled hard at her, and turned around towards it. I could hear her tiniest breath behind me. She was breathing like a child and not like the plump woman she was. The crunch of gravel was like the roar of traffic beside that sound. We scraped past the oak doors and between a medley of huge sprawling trees. Two enormous conifers flanked the main path, casting cool bogeymen shadows which followed us into the small doorway at the back of the church. I had to duck, but the woman was shorter. I wondered, *is she scared?* Because I heard her hesitation, that quick suck in of air before she rested her hands on the damp slate, then followed me in.

<u>Shona</u>
I can't help watching her from the doorway. I can't help watching all of us. I wish Hugo would hurry up. I know he's almost with us because I can hear very clearly the sounds of people in the main hall. Melanie crouches at the woman's feet, and gesticulates wildly with both hands. She's talking at the woman in a low voice, too low for me to catch the words. The woman doesn't lift her head up, or answer, or make any noise at all. I'm resting against the doorframe and the wood is cool against my back. I realise suddenly that I must look like a cow writhing at an itch below my shoulder, so I swing round and down into the chair facing the woman.
  'What's your name?'
  The woman keeps her head down.
  'What's your name?'
I can see the woman looking through her hair at my long bony hands. Short nails and narrow wedding band. I smother my left hand with my right and she looks back down at her own feet. I can't believe how broad the woman's feet are, clumsy in gleaming white trainers. Her legs are bare, brown, and covered in thin dark hairs which are blonder at the ends, there's a deep graze down one shin which she rubs at gently. I can hear Melanie

sucking loudly on a mint, and find my eyes closing for a second before trying —

'Where do you come from?'

The room smells fusty. In one low corner, where a beam runs in a downwards curve into the wall, a box of old books rots slowly. The woman watches Melanie slide the packet of polos onto the table. The packet is torn, and silver glints dangerously in the half-light.

'We won't hurt you, we want to help. What is your name?'

'She can't understand you. You're scaring her.'

Melanie's whisper is breathy, youthful and it makes me flinch; so I lean over the table with my hands spread to steady myself. I'm sure I can hear her muttering. What is she saying? I'm straining to catch the words through Melanie's excited voice which is filling the room. Hugo's here, I can tell. But it doesn't matter, because I've got it, I've heard. I flick dust from my sleeve and turn and say —

'Paola...her name's Paola.'

'A refugee!' hisses Melanie.

M

The moon is very bright tonight, and I can hear crickets whirring in the grass around me. The air is cool and I am calm enough, I think, to consider today. Dominic came. His face was red and puffy, he has been drinking for courage again. He would not believe me when I said I knew it was his birthday. Why must he argue? His voice all thin and brittle, not in the least bit slurry —

'You could have sent a card!'

I said 'I knew you'd come,' and he looked away with *that* look. He did not believe me, that's for certain. He thought I'd forgotten. I wish I *could* forget. But he would not believe me, and I shouted at him, that is true.

He called for the supervisor who sniffs too loudly. I could have throttled him gently with two hands, so perhaps I am not really calm enough, yet. It is difficult when he looks at me that way, with his eyes somewhere else, and he is sad. He walks around me with his back straight and does that thing with his fingers which drives me insane. I still felt angry, and cold somehow, that he would not believe me, until he dipped to say goodbye, and then I could not help but squeeze him tight, tighter than I should perhaps, although he would not look at me. Then he left.

I put his card in the bin. I did not need to prove the point, tonight. The woman with the sniff brought it, and apologised. She could not find one that said *'brother'*. Despite that — after all, he can hardly complain, I cannot get out to shop myself — I gave her fifty-nine pence for it in shiny coppers. Her skirt rattled strangely with it all afternoon, oh well, whatever. It is cooler still now. I shall go and retrieve my cardigan, come back out, then listen to the crickets and the other snuffling creatures. The man in the moon is looking pensive, and perhaps if I sit here and sing *claire de la lune*, and think of Dominic, then I may cry a little in this bright-lit dark.

M

This evening at 'tea' — mush, mush and more mush — a strange sound tormented me throug hout. It was one of those sounds which niggles away, insistent and repetitive, I could not guess it until after the meal, when they turned off that damned radio and the cutlery and dentures had stopped their nauseating clanking. And yes, I am angry again tonight. Yes, but that is another story.

I was pretending to read in the corner by the window — to ward off the new girl with the giggles — and to keep out half a watch for Dominic, in case he should come, which he didn't — when this noise began again. It seemed close to my ear, and it was definitely a buzz. A large, fat fly — a bootleblue — was caught in a web, in the bottom left-hand corner of the window. The spider was tiny, less than half the fly's size, but it trapped the fly and ate it. The fly buzzed and buzzed, until after it was half-eaten. I could hardly believe how long it buzzed. I stopped looking to make good the pretence of reading and got hooked on a page about the Herault. When I looked back, the spider and the fly had gone. So I read some more, and now I cannot be certain why I am angry this evening, except it is something to do with Dominic, and that much is true.

Valerie Laws

Maas en meisjes

The brochures are full of them; Dutch girls,
Gouda-gold hair, skin plump and creamy
as a young cow's udder,
their heads tipped back.
They love those fish,
raw, marinated herrings, gutted.
No chocolate flakes that soften
in the mouth for these Amazons,
no scented baths and ringing phones,
but the stiff, supple, silver bolt
sliding salty between their parted lips
as red and round as Edam cheeses
and down those strong white throats,
swallowed whole.

Why me?

One day
you find a spider on your towel,
starred black into the fabric;
after that it's always there,
crouching,
to be found again.

Once you've met the man in the alley,
smelt his breath, known the spades of his hands,
his footsteps patrol
your dreams.

Once you've felt the impact of metal,
seen the road spin round you,
you feel the shock as every car you pass

hits you,
a flinching in the gut.

You've been skinned like meat,
stripped of that invisible membrane
which keeps you immune
until it's punctured, shredded, lost,
exposing your flesh to the truth:
there is no 'why me?'

There is only 'why not?'

River blindness

Unlike our crops, we grow towards the dark.
The names of things we taste like fruit
held in the mouth, a scent
hinting at the shapes our memories hold.
The river is twisted rope
burning our hands as we feel our way,
hearing the sun flash
on endless skeins of water.
Growing older is learning to walk
daily more slowly,
using our ever-tasting hands,
groping into blackness.
We learn to let our children lead us,
lean on them, the smooth pebbles
of their shoulders warm under our fingers.
Our feet learn to stumble,
our toes smell the way
like the snouts of pigs
truffling through the dust.
Food is a warm breath on the face.
The brown drone of flies, the violet call of birds,
tickle our skin. We grow down,
seeking the darkness of roots coiling,
the comfort of heartbeat, holding our children's faces
sealed under our eyelids.

Joanna Curtis
Turning Soft
from a novel in progress

She used to wear little silver earrings which chinked against each other if she moved her head suddenly. He couldn't remember how many, but a lot of thin silver rings with tiny objects, stars, sickle moons, a miniature unicorn, hanging from them. She didn't have anything else pierced, just her ears, and only the soft part of the lobe, so there can't have been that many. He remembered the just audible tinkle of them as she turned over in bed. He used to wonder, did the stars stick into her when she lay on her side? She never took them off. But it didn't stop her sleeping.

Why should he remember her now? He sat at the table with the early pale light just enough to see by, and his appetite for breakfast had gone. He had been up two hours already. He rolled crumbs of cold toast between his thumb and fingers and looked at nothing.

It must be six, seven years? That would make his son almost ten. He didn't know where they were and he told himself he didn't care. The boy probably had a new daddy now, he thought; more than likely. They probably lived in a town; she was always a townie, really, squeamish about a lot of things. Critical, too — moaned about the lack of cinemas and supermarkets, that sort of thing. It occurred to him that he didn't want his son brought up to have the same attitude. It must have been seeing Tim and his boy yesterday, that's what bought this mood on. Tim had been showing something to him, and the boy was taking notice. But there was no point thinking his son could be like that; too late, now.

Judd drank his tea and shrugged himself into his coat again. It was a shapeless thing, smelling of wax and earth with pockets which bulged whether they were empty or full. When he went out, he was followed silently by a handsome spaniel and a humpity-backed, spindle-legged terrier with a thin, sharp head.

The pheasant chicks were like a soft brown sea, surging forward as he scattered grain. Sometimes he'd let them out of the pen, and they'd follow him about the wood as if he was their mother. Stupid little things. Bred to be shot, but at least they weren't kept in a box like battery chickens. A lot of meat on a pheasant, if you liked the taste. He threw more grain and shut the pen. Soon they'd be let out to fend for themselves. A late batch, these, too late, really, and too puny to be shot this season. It was amazing how many of them dodged the guns, considering their incredible stupidity. Perhaps it was because the very dim ones never seemed to learn to fly, just ran through the undergrowth. They couldn't be shot if they didn't fly, could they? Maybe they weren't so dim. Pheasants could run surprisingly fast. He stopped walking abruptly. Now that's the sort of thing he should be telling his lad. He should be here, my son.

The trees swayed around him. He came to a clearing where he saw a couple of magpies squabbling over something dead. He raised his gun, but the young springer started forward and they flew noisily away. 'No!' he said, and cuffed the dog sharply on the muzzle. 'Daft bugger.' It cowered, turning its yellow eyes on him with a look of reproach and apology mixed. 'You've got to learn,' he added. The dog wagged its tail briefly. I'm turning soft, he thought.

The corpse was a young badger. He nudged it over with his foot; it had not been dead long. He saw the lice and fleas still crawling through the coarse grey hairs. The magpies had done little damage; it seemed asleep. Its eyes were closed, the black edges tight together. He lifted the black leather lip to expose the wicked white teeth. The grey snout reminded him of an old terrier he'd once known. He reckoned the badger had been hit by a car while crossing one of the roads that bordered the estate. He manipulated each leg in turn, and found one to be broken. Bound to have been a car, then. It must have crawled a mile at least after it was hit. Brave, badgers were. Fighters, too. He straightened, thinking what a shame it had to die that way. When he was about ten, the same age that his son was now, an unscrupulous uncle had taken him to an illegal fight between a badger and some dogs. His parents had never found out where he'd been, but wondered what had upset him so much. His mother went on about it for ages, but he never told them why he had been so pale and silent after that outing with his uncle. At least one dog had died. It sickened him, and his uncle had called him soft and had never taken him anywhere again. But he always kept a close eye on the sets in the wood for signs of human interference.

He called the dogs, who had shown no interest in the body after the first perfunctory sniff, and started off towards where he'd seen part of the fence broken down. He'd phone the badger people later, if he remembered. He'd had them down as interfering do-gooders, but some of them were okay. The bloke he usually spoke to lived in the village and sometimes drank in the local. He was all right.

That evening he had a bath and lit candles, like she used to do. If his mates could see him they'd think he was a poof. He kept the candles in case of a power cut, plain white ones — none of hers were left. They'd bathe together, often, in the Victorian bath she'd spotted in a field being used as a water trough. Sometimes the baby would come into the bath, too, smacking the water with his starfish hands. It was coming up to the boy's tenth birthday, soon, and his own fortieth. It made you think, that. Forty, and what had he got? The cottage wasn't even his. As he wallowed in the steaming water, the spindle-legged terrier trotted into the bathroom and put its front paws on the edge of the bath. It panted at him, a wicked, grinning face like a gargoyle, and tried to lap the water. Then it went out, leaving the door gaping and letting cold air in. 'I wish you'd learn to shut the door, you little sod!' Heaving himself up, Judd leant at a perilous angle and managed to swing the door to. He'd kept the dogs inside since she'd left. When the old springer had died, he'd got this one; never lived outside. House dogs, now, both of them. But they did their work, not like pampered town dogs. He kept a handful of chickens in the old dog pen. They used to have the run of the garden, but the foxes had visited too often.

Foxes; that reminded him. He said he'd help out at the kennels when Bob Downie went in to get his hernia fixed — that must be quite soon. He quite liked being at the kennels, he almost went in for it as a job, but gamekeeping was what he was destined to do. It's what his dad had done until he'd broken his back falling off a roof. The old man had eventually managed to walk again, with the aid of two sticks, but he couldn't work.

Turning Soft

He must have been, what, forty-five, when the accident had happened. Judd, the second son, had been fifteen, the same age as his son would be when he was forty-five. Dad had got very old very quickly, after that. He was only fifty-eight when he died, but at least he'd seen one of his children follow in his footsteps. Just. Gave you a sense of continuity, that. Mentally he shook himself. Must stop dwelling on the boy. Could be anywhere, could be in Australia for all he knew, except that a couple of years ago someone told him (he never asked how they knew) that the boy and his mother were living in Manchester. Still wounded by their departure, he had not followed it up. Too proud.

He let the water out of the bath and climbed out, catching sight of himself as he did so in the big mirror which hung over the bath. An ornate thing, with stained and spotted glass, she'd picked it up at a junk shop. By candle-light, with the mirror partly steamed over, he didn't look too bad for a bloke of nearly forty. Hadn't run to fat due to his job being so active, still got his hair . . . Judd remembered a girl he went out with when he was sixteen, just before he went away. She was older than him and the first girl to let him sleep with her. Carol, her name was, and she had said that he was the sort to improve with age. At the time, he was a bit insulted, thinking she meant he was immature. Funny how he'd never forgotten that, yet he couldn't recall the actual sex with any clarity, and they said you never forgot your first.

Fucking, screwing, shagging. So important when you'd never done it, you burned for it, it ate you up. Then you had it, and it wasn't quite what you'd thought, but you wanted it again. He found after the first taste that he could get girls quite easily, but the sort that were just for fucking, not the ones you wanted to talk to.

He hadn't slept with a woman for almost two years. He wasn't old, so perhaps he wasn't normal. He'd become less confident with women, couldn't summon the energy or the courage to go through the old chat-up routine. His desires were still there, they had not deserted him, but they were buried under layers of thought. He did a lot of thinking. He was known as a bit of a loner. Never used to be. Right now he could go out and catch last orders at the pub, but he preferred to put some music on, or watch TV. for a bit. Sometimes he might do a bit of reading, he'd got quite into those fantasy books about other worlds, and he liked ones about history. He'd never read when he was younger. Never seemed to have the time, too busy doing things or just mucking around. Judd wondered if his son read at all.

'He'll have to go soon,' Dave, one of the kennelmen, pointed out a tall, pale-coloured hound. It had a battle-scarred appearance; years of running through undergrowth and bickering over food had left its face flecked with old scars, and one of its ears was torn. 'Shame. He was most often the leader, but he injured a paw last season and it never mended right. Still strong as the others, but I doubt he'll manage to keep up. We'll see how he goes tomorrow.'

Judd looked closely at the hound. 'I walked that one,' he said, recognizing it. 'Not that old, is he?'

'Seven is all, should've had two or three good years in him, at least, but it's that paw. Always went at it hell for leather, that's the problem.'

Judd remembered how he'd agreed to walk the hound puppy after he'd taken his boy to see the litter. The child had waded into the melee of puppies, quite unafraid, and picked up a lemon-coloured one which had squirmed and squeaked and licked his face. The hound had been returned to the pack only a month before she had taken the boy away.

'Yeah, it is a shame,' he said, meaning the hound.

'He's no good to himself if he can't keep up with the others.'

'I'll do it.'

'What?'

'Shoot him, if it's needed.'

Dave shrugged. 'Well, you're officially working here, aren't you, so that's fine by me. It's not a job I like, anyway. Won't make no odds to him, either.'

Liz Sampson

Shearing

I watched and listened.
That's how I learned
to fleece like them.
To strip away
the bulky woolly covering,
and reveal the body beneath.
Always surprised,
at how small it was.
Defenceless,
blue veins showing,
bloodspots,
where the shears slipped.

Eileen Jones

The Stray

At first I didn't notice
the stray who sneaked in with you
though I sensed her furry kiss
and then a blurred
skulking at the edge,
which resolved, as she grew bolder,
into something sharp.
But I was charmed of course:
she was flighty, quick,
keen to please.
Only later did she show her teeth and claws;
by then I couldn't make her leave.

When I stopped feeding her
she began to tear my skin
though her eyes were gentle, pleading.
I keep her hidden now.
Her presence is forbidden
and I know she wants to mark you,
to weave herself
around you.
'It isn't on,' I tell her, trying to explain.
She stares back dumbly, unsheathes her claws.
I should save my breath —
she's only heard her name, and yours.

Off Line
(after Louis MacNeice)

Say that she's having a word —
not life or death — with no one special
maybe some bloke at work
and then her light goes out. She's off
into some mental shopping mall
to lift a few small items for a laugh.

But other times she's in his face
more than he might expect.
As if the goods she wants to liberate
are his. As if she gives herself the right
to come round and collect
after she's tracked him down one night.

It's out of order all of this.
It can't go on. She gets a grip
and locks her eyes on his
to let him know her mind is back on line.
But still her thoughts and eyes might dip
improperly, from time to time.

Pru Kitching

Small pebbles

Sometimes there is more magic around. Iced, black trees and a moon-crazed hare, racing the Fiesta and beating it. And the Ave Marie Stella sky like five pence pieces in a sugar jar. The dogs feel it first, then the horses and then other animals. Man last. Dullard.

by...

There is an agitation like the sudden arrival of power or dressing in jewel colours before setting off for the orgy. All finery, she looks like the Queen of Sheba, he like Benjamin Disraeli. I, in my one green wellie and single glass slipper, do not, it appears, fit in.

the river...

He dives through the glass as a mallard would splash through green splinters to take his bath. Knowingly, his feathers are oil-free, his trunks Speedo. He drowns anyway in his own cash. Shacked up, crammed in, cracked down into his spleen. And so he knows how bad it is.

Andrea Russell
Mouse

One of the kittens died, named Mouse. Named Mouse because it was so small. It was mostly black except for white feet and stomach, and its dark nose had one tiny spot of pink on the tip, so it looked like a mouse's small pointed nose. He was always smaller than the rest, the other five, but not that much smaller.

When they were born, I was surprised by the amount of blood and the smell. I remembered our previous cat's kittens and they seemed to come out with little effort and not much mess. This was different.

I watched her — her name was Dusty — go into Paul's closet. Paul is my son. He's eleven. I put an old mattress pad down and waited. She began breathing hard, down through her contractions, and I wondered if it would get bad. I remembered how I didn't know what labour would be like, my first time. Did she have any inkling of what was happening? Her sighs grew heavier and she shuddered as she bore down. One bad moment happened when she jumped up, leapt around and picked up a green pushpin from the floor. She started chewing it furiously. I grew afraid but then she lay down, and the first kitten was born. About half an hour later, another. By noon there were six. I was surprised the way they just kept coming. First litters are usually not bigger than three.

Paul and I stood in the door of the closet, looking at the kittens, the blood, a wad of placenta about four inches long. 'Phew,' Paul said. 'It stinks.' I changed the mat, put another one down.

At first the kittens looked pretty much the same, but in a few days we could tell the difference between them and began to name them. Suzanne, my second child, named Mouse 'Mouse'. He seemed fine, just a little small. 'There's always a runt,' I said. We laughed at its efforts to push its splayed pink toes, ridiculously small and sweet, and its claws, as thin as threads, to the mother's nipples. 'Look how small he is, he's so cute.' I was sure he was all right, just the runt.

About three weeks later, Claire, my oldest, came to me. 'I'm worried about Mouse,' she said. She's fifteen, and the most sensible. 'He doesn't look good.' I came to look. She was right. Its eyes were blue and foggy and not open all the way. I could feel its ribs. It was more like a baby bird than a kitten.

I called the vet. 'It's not getting enough food,' he said right off. 'Feed it Pablum.' I bought some, and with a coffee spoon smeared a bit on its mouth. Nothing. No reaction. That night I looked in on them in the closet and only counted five. Dusty, I found, was sitting on Mouse, squashing it in the corner. I took it out from under her but its head flopped over to one side, out of control, no longer able to lift that heavy weight. The fur on the back of its head was thin, like a balding man's. I was angry with the mother for giving up.

I thought it would be so nice to have kittens. Such a good experience for the children.

'Well, that's nature,' my husband Charles said.

'You can't just let it die,' said Paul.

At a quarter to ten that night I wrapped it in an old yellowing undershirt of Charles's, put it next to my skin under my red sweatshirt and drove to the vet's.

He was just the runt. I never thought it would die. Maybe he was a defective kitten right from the start and never would have made it.

The vet gave me cat formula, a syringe and paediatric vitamins, and told me to feed it every two hours. First I put it in my top dresser drawer, but it mewed and tried to climb out. So I put it with the mother and hoped that she wouldn't sit on it again.

I went to bed at midnight, up at two, four, again at six. It fed eagerly, lapping at the tip of the syringe. I began to gather energy. I would save it.

By morning it was better, its eyes brighter — but in the afternoon, it started to fade. It stopped eating. The fur under its chin was hard with dried milk. Its eyes narrowed, grew more cloudy, one less open than the other. Nevertheless, I kept trying to squeeze the tip of the syringe into the side of its mouth. The milk would trickle out the sides. I heard a little clicking sound each time it inhaled.

It was dying for sure.

Nevertheless, I kept it wrapped. Kept putting it up against the mother. Nevertheless, it didn't feed.

I wrapped it in a towel. I put it back in the drawer. It was now too weak to climb out. I heard it mew a couple of times in the night. I got out of bed and put my ear down close to the drawer. I could still hear the clicks.

It was dead in the morning. And each of my children said, 'Are you sure?'

'Are you sure?'

'Are you sure?'

I showed them the stiff, matted paws, and the mouth like a fish; the eyes open, one more than the other. Death, you're always the same. The life fades, fades, fades and is gone, somewhere, somewhere, where? Little kitten, I'm so sorry, I'm so sorry. 'What if this was its only chance?' said Paul. 'Three weeks and it's over.' It was an unbearable thought. 'I think it's going to get reincarnated as another kitten,' he said.

'I bet you're right,' I said. But oh, I think it's my fault. And I'm trying to understand why I care so much. I'm aware of the maudlin silliness of it all. How in the world did people manage in the old days to survive the death of children? How do they manage now? Trying to get them to feed and watching that life drain away like water in a tub, like a violin's sound getting thinner, thinner, you strain to hear it — it's gone.

We buried it. Paul dug a hole next to Big T, our earlier cat. Paul got out one of the shoeboxes for his fancy running shoes. 'Air Walk Cool Cat,' it said. It was even black and white, like Mouse. Perfect. It had a round hole cut in the side, for some previous cat game. I plugged the hole with Kleenex.

We put it in the ground. 'Do you want to look at it?' I asked. They all did.

We closed the lid, covered it up. Paul went back to skateboarding. I put lilac cuttings in the earth, mounding up the soil to make the flowers stand up. A proper grave. And went in to fix dinner.

The smell of stew came out of the kitchen wall vent just to the left of the grave when I went out to look again, crying again. Crazy. Crying for all dead children, for mine that could be dead, but aren't, and for the parents who, I am sure, really do try their best; even mine, my own dead parents — in the ground, too.

Jo McCullock
Camper

The bell rings three times. I check that everything is secure in the room and put Tom's present in the rucksack before throwing it over my shoulder. The bell rings again.

'How you doing?' I ask, struggling through the door.

Tom stands there, his hands shoved deep into his pockets. He looks me up and down, failing to hide his surprise.

'You've shaved your head,' I say to break the awkward silence.

He shrugs. He looks younger, smaller, like a teenager. I dwarf him with my height and my bulk. I lug the bag through the sliding door of the camper, red in the face from the activity. Tom watches, frowning.

'Supplies!' I say, cheerily, as the bottles of beer clink against each other.

The van is small. There's a couch covered in Dralon and a sink as big as a cereal bowl. A string of gold tinsel is pinned around the window.

'Come on, John,' he says, 'I'll show you round.' Tom jumps in and I follow. 'What do you think?' he asks, smiling.

'It's great,' I say, 'compact. Where shall I put my sleeping bag?' I try to be tactful.

From above the windows he pulls out a bed suspended to the wall. It looks like a child's hammock. As I wonder how I'll fit my massive frame in, he opens the seat and proudly shows me a fold-up mattress.

'You can sleep on this. You could fit a whole family in here.'

I smile at his optimism. Maybe he hasn't changed that much, just a little older. I move up to the front and he starts the engine. Icy air blowing gale force into my face.

'It'll warm up in a minute,' he reassures me.

I pull my scarf tightly round my face and say in a muffled voice, 'This is going to be great, just like being seventeen again.'

Tom grins and cranks the camper into gear. It stalls. He swears and restarts the engine. Although it is only lunchtime, it's nearly dark; the road lit up by Christmas lights from people's windows. I take the map from my pocket as we drive onto the motorway. Tom is quiet. He likes to concentrate when he drives. I settle back into my seat.

'So where are we heading first?' I ask. Tom shrugs as I list a number of places that I have ringed on my map. Whenever we'd travelled together in the past I always decided.

'I don't really want to go too far up in one day,' he says, 'somewhere in the lowlands, maybe on the coast.'

Impatiently, I suck air between my teeth, I want excitement but he peers ahead at the shiny road, a route in mind. 'OK, wherever you think.' I look at him, willing him to speak; he waves to a passing camper, the same make as his own, but still says nothing. 'So what have you been up to?'

'Not much, overtime mostly.'

'Oh.' I wait for him to carry on; he wasn't usually this quiet. Maybe our friendship has been on hold for too long. After a couple of minutes I ask after his family. He tells me they're fine. He doesn't ask after mine, although I'd written at the end of the summer and told him that my Dad had died.

'It'll be good to get away from it all,' I say, thinking of my central heating and watching Christmas movies on my wide screen television, 'just like old times.'

Tom bites his lip. 'I couldn't stand another Christmas dinner with my Mum and Dad. Interfering bastards.'

I'm taken aback by the poison in his voice and my stomach knots as I realise that I won't get a chance to spend Christmas with my parents again. 'Why don't you move out?' I say, knowing that I suggest this every time I see him.

He gives me a sideways look, like it's none of my business.

Sleet hits the windscreen and I inspect my watch. 'When do you want to stop?' I ask.

'Dunno, see how the weather goes.'

I pull my coat tighter.

'There are some Mars bars in the glove compartment,' says Tom, his eyes never shifting from the road. I unwrap one and hand it to him, taking the other for myself.

'Have you been out much?' I ask, my mouth full of the sickly chocolate.

'I went to the Catholic Club with my Dad on Saturday. Had a few pints.' He nibbles at his chocolate bar, like a squirrel with a nut.

The camper does a steady fifty miles an hour and my eyes start to drop as I listen to the chugging of the engine. When I wake up, Tom is pulling into a garage. As I rub my dead nose, he jumps out with energy.

'There's a coffee machine inside.'

I slap my arms and gingerly open the door, sharp air cutting into my face. As Tom fills the camper with petrol, I make my way over to the garage shop. Apart from the hot drink machine, the shop hasn't been modernised for decades. Bottles of oil and antifreeze are displayed on the shelf behind the till. The only food I can spy is a jar of lollipops on the counter. An old man sits reading. I go to the drink machine and put in some money. It comes out. I try it again.

'It takes tokens,' says the old man.

I grit my teeth and walk over to the counter where he gives me two tokens.

'There's only tomato soup left,' he says. I can tell by his accent that we are in Scotland. I clutch two cups of powdery soup as Tom comes in to pay.

'There's a place we can camp about fifteen miles up the road.'

I nod, sipping at the tepid liquid. Tom's sits on the dashboard forming a skin. Off the motorway, the road is black; the moon reflecting off the snow topped trees. A couple of cars pass by, each travelling twice our speed. I rub my grumbling stomach as the acidity of the soup comes into my mouth.

'There's a little stove in the back, we can make something when we park up.' Tom grins.

I look behind to see where it could be hidden. The headlights pick out a road sign.

'Not far now,' says Tom. He swerves to the left and drives down a dirt track. The camper bumps up and down. 'Nearly missed it,' he says, his eyes concentrating on the black ahead.

'Do you know where we're going?' I ask. There are no signs or landmarks to be seen, and it is too dark to check my map.

'Just have faith, will you?' His tone is harsh, so I shut my mouth and wait. The trees above are so dense that even the moon has disappeared. He turns to the right and stops. 'Here we are,' he says, grinning.

Looking out of the window, I doubt how he could know. There is nothing to be seen.

'Shall we have a look round?' Tom asks as he turns off the engine. Then he smiles, seeing the reluctance on my face. 'Only kiddin', we've got all day tomorrow for that.'

Turning the light on, he climbs in the back, and I follow clumsily. I sit down waiting for instructions, but Tom starts pulling food from cupboards and out of his rucksack. He turns, a loaf in one hand and a can of beans in the other.

'You'll have to move, the stove is there,' he says, flipping up a piece of Formica to reveal two gas rings and a grill. Shuffling along the seat, I pull out my map, whilst Tom busies himself with supper. The light is dim and as he moves, huge shadows are cast over me. I use my torch to follow the route we have taken, worried about where we are. I shut the map impatiently as I see that our off-road route is the tiniest squiggle on the page.

Tom hands me a cup of strong tea. It tastes like it has come from a flask. I sip it anyway. He reaches behind my head, and I duck as he pulls down the tabletop, pinning me into my seat. He sits next to me and we eat quickly and in silence.

'We'll wash these in the morning,' he says, putting the dirty dishes into a plastic bag. Lighting some tealights, he places them carefully around the camper. As they twinkle, it begins to feel homely, still cosy from the heat of the grill. Tom slumps besides me.

'Have you brought something to read?'

I nod, aware that I am touching him. He pulls a book from his pocket, its cover cracked from being folded.

'That's not your usual reading material?' I can only see the word 'magic' in the title and assume that it's a fantasy novel.

Tom looks furtive. 'It was a present.'

'Who from?'

'A girl.'

'What girl?'

'Someone I've met.' He looks flushed.

'Well obviously, but who? What's her name?' I feel like I'm grilling him.

'Her name's Linda, she works in the Co-op,' he smiles.

I want to ask more but don't. I smile back and flick through the back of the map looking for places of interest. Tom is waiting for my next question. I can feel him staring at me. I look up.

Sighing I say, 'Well go on, give us the details.'

He looks at his book, nervously flicking the pages. Sometimes he is such a big kid.

'How did you meet?'

'When I was shopping.'

'Oh right.'

'Anyway, I kept popping in to see her. It was costing me a fortune 'cos I had to buy something every time I went in. The cat has never been so well fed,' he laughs and I smile in encouragement.

'Have you been out with her?'

'Not yet, but only because she's been working so much and her Dad's a bit over-protective.' It pours from his mouth as he sees the interest drain from my face.

'Why, how old is she?'

'Eighteen,' he squeaks.

I whistle under my breath. 'You could almost be her Dad, at a push.'

'Don't be daft,' he fidgets with the cord on his trousers.

'So basically, you've met her in the shop when she's been working?'

'Yeah.'

'Have you asked her out?'

'No.'

I turn back to my map, thinking of Tom's previous obsessions. Nothing real ever became of them. I glance at him as he shifts sulkily towards the window.

'So, did you buy Linda a Christmas present?' I ask, bored with the icy atmosphere.

'Yeah, a Robbie Williams CD and a pair of socks.' He looks over and smiles, 'but she hasn't opened them yet.'

'I don't suppose she could while she was working,' I joke. His face twists in contempt and he looks like he wants to kill me. I bury my head in my map, but I can still feel his eyes burning into my skin.

The next morning I wake up, desperately wanting the toilet. The radio is on low and the camper is moving. I pull myself from the sleeping bag to wipe the steamy window. Snow has fallen overnight and there is a light covering on the trees. The road is wet. The rustling of the sleeping bag has told Tom I am awake but he doesn't speak. I make my way to the passenger seat, rubbing colour into my cheeks.

'Where are we going?' I ask. He doesn't answer. 'Tom?'

'Wait and see,' he laughs.

'I need the loo.' Again he ignores me. 'Tom, will you just tell me where we are going or at least how long it will be 'til we get there?'

'I said wait and see.' Biting his bottom lip, he looks ahead at the road.

'I thought the idea of this trip was that we both decided where we wanted to go.' My face is almost touching his but he refuses to look. I turn the radio off in anger. Tom switches it back on, but raises the volume so that crackly pop music booms from his decrepit speakers.

'Just stop,' I shout at him, tempted to pull at the handbrake for a moment. He grips the steering wheel firmly and I stand, making my way to the back. As I get to my rucksack, Tom applies the brakes and I fall heavily into the cupboard.

'We're here,' he says cheerily, as I lie in a daze.

'You fuckin' idiot,' I mutter, rubbing my swollen head.

Tom jumps through to the back. 'You've cut yourself,' he says inspecting my face, and hands me a piece of kitchen roll, 'you should be more careful when we're movin'.'

'What is wrong with you?' I ask, dabbing the bridge of my nose. There's some blood.

'Me? You're the one who got up in a strop.' He pulls his coat on as I struggle to my feet. 'I don't remember you being this bad in the morning.' He slides the door open.

Grabbing my coat and toilet bag, I step out of the camper into a tiny car park. Toms locks up and heads to where a sign points 'Town Centre'. I follow him slowly, dizzy from my fall.

'The toilets are there,' Tom points to a small stone building hidden by shops. 'I'll see you in an hour, there's some things I have to get.'

'I won't be that long,' I shout, but he's already walking across the road. He waves without turning his head. Sighing, I make my way to the toilets where the stone floor smells of disinfectant and I shave without being disturbed.

Heading into the street, I check my watch, another forty minutes to kill. Wandering past the bus station, I think of another day spent with Tom and my stomach turns. Out of interest I go into the tiny booking office and check the timetable. There's one coach a week and it went yesterday.

'Not trying to escape, are we?' says Tom as I come out.

'Do you think we've enough food?' I ask, trying to change the subject.

'Probably,' he mutters.

Back at the camper I offer to wash the dishes to keep Tom in a good mood.

'Did them this morning, before you woke up,' he says, as I look for the bag of plates. He hands me a banana and an apple. 'Breakfast,' he says, and I eat them even though I don't like bananas.

'So where now,' I ask, taking my place in the passenger seat, map in hand.

'I thought you had somewhere in mind.'

I point to the map and Tom virtually snatches it from me.

'It'll take ages to get there.' His face is scrunched up.

'It'll take two hours, two and a half at the most,' I say, wishing I could drive. Tom studies the map, turning it about in his hands like it's a complicated route.

'I'll direct you, we won't get lost.'

He looks grumpy and says, 'I'll drive for two hours and see where we are then.' I sigh resignedly, fed up of the bickering.

There's a quiz on the radio and I join in, glad of the distraction. Pretty soon Tom is answering questions. We laugh about all the stupid things that have happened in the past year. The two hours fly and I trace the map.

'We're nearly there,' I say, 'there should be a car park about a hundred yards up.' Tom slows down but there is no car park, just a gate with a big chain round it.

'Looks like they closed it, for some reason,' says Tom, a smug look on his face. 'We'll just park here.' He steers the camper to the side of the road and turns the engine off.

The mountains stretch in front of us, snow peaked and green at the same time. We silently admire the view. Pulling on our walking boots and coats, we head towards them, knowing that there are only two hours of daylight left.

We get back to the camper just as the light fades. The air is heavy with frost but we are hot from walking, sweaty almost. He puts the kettle on the gas ring and I pull out some biscuits. We sit munching, waiting for the kettle's whistle.

We play 'Pontoon', first for biscuits and then for copper. I try to remember card games that I played as a child, but only their names are there, Old Maid, Donkey; I've no idea of the rules. After a while Tom says that he doesn't want to run the battery down using the light, so we doze, tired from the walk.

There's a crunch of footsteps and I stir suddenly as someone raps on the window. I can see the whites of Tom's eyes. As I adjust to the dark, he puts his finger to his mouth. The person outside raps on the window again, but much harder this time.

'Hello, is anyone in there?' The voice sounds friendly and I stand to open the door.

'Don't,' hisses Tom, but I ignore him, a madman wouldn't knock. Sliding the door back, I see a policeman standing in the road.

'Sorry to disturb you,' he says in a soft accent. I breathe out and beckon to Tom.

'I passed earlier and noticed that there was no one here.'

'We were out walking,' says Tom, aggressively.

'Thought so, just making sure you were back safe, those hills are pretty dangerous after dark, there's been a few go missing.' The policeman smiles.

'Thanks,' I say. Tom looks sullen.

'Well, as long as you're all right.' He walks over to his car and radios through.

'I thought he was going to move us on,' says Tom, slamming the door and putting the light on again.

'It was nice of him to check on us,' I say.

Tom curls his lip and mutters, 'Money for old rope.'

We sit at the window as the sleet falls. Tom passes me a shot of whisky in a cup and I gulp it back, burning my throat but feeling instantly flushed.

Flicking through maps, we talk about the places we have been together over the years. Camping in the Lake District when we were teenagers, inter- railing in our early twenties. I feel sad that our friendship has lapsed over the years but as the whisky takes effect I begin to think that we could make more of an effort. We finish off the bottle and fall into unconsciousness.

I stir from my sleep the next morning to see that snow has gathered in the corners of the windows. I think how festive it looks and turn to Tom, but his sleeping bag is empty. As I put my jumper on, he comes through the door waving a load of holly.

'Great,' I say unenthusiastically, as my brain pounds from last night's alcohol.

'Just trying to get into the Christmas spirit,' he mutters.

'Where are we off today then?' I keep my voice cheery, aware of Tom's moods. Shrugging, he puts the kettle on. I feel tense. He makes the tea in silence and heads to the driver's seat. As he starts the engine, I make my way up to the front. We drive for about ten minutes and he stops at an old red phone box. He turns to me.

'I have to ring Linda,' he says and I bite my lip. 'She gave me her phone number.' He waves a scrap of paper in front of my face. Eagerly, he jumps from the camper and I watch as he goes to the phone box. He dials and gives me the thumbs up. I rub my chin, aware that I need to shave. After about ten minutes, he puts the phone down and comes back in.

'So what did she say?' I ask.

He glares at me, his face flushed. 'This and that, what she's been up to.'

'Was she glad you rang?' I ask.

'What is this? Twenty questions?'

'Just making conversation,' I say. His eyes dart from my left eye to my right. He starts the engine.

'Get in the back', he says as I rub my hands together.

'I'm OK,' I say.

He turns to me, his eyes narrow. 'You're disturbing my concentration.'

'But I'm not doing anything.'

'John, just get in the back. It's my camper.' His voice is low but vicious. I go to the back and although it's still morning, I climb into my sleeping bag, glad of its comfort. Tom drives back to where we stayed last night. I shiver uncomfortably. It's eleven a.m. by my watch. I go over and touch his arm.

'Tom, what do you want to do?'

He wipes my hand away like it's a piece of dust and hisses, 'Get back.' I sigh loudly to let him know I'm annoyed, but he doesn't flinch. I zip my sleeping bag around me and wait. Tom doesn't move. I can see him staring into space. Despite my sleeping bag I'm cold. It begins to snow again. I take out some oatcakes and cheese. I ask Tom if he wants anything but he doesn't reply. He doesn't move.

After lunch I go outside to pee. A thin layer of snow has covered the ground and it turns to powder as I walk upon it. Making my way behind a tree, I think that Tom will probably help himself to lunch whilst I am gone. However when I return he is still in the same position. I put my Walkman on.

Two CDs later Tom still hasn't moved. I want to plead with him but his silence worries me. It's dark and the camper is a deep freeze. Tom hasn't eaten or spoken all day. I stare hard to see if he is still alive. The fog coming from his mouth tells me that he is.

I pull a flapjack from my rucksack. 'Tom, you should have something to eat,' I shout, but if he hears he doesn't respond. I eat it myself, needing the sugar and fat for energy. I start to move around, rubbing my legs, the circulation slowly returning. I make a noise as I bang into things, but Tom gives no sign that he has noticed. Once my legs feel alive again, I return to the sleeping bag, waiting.

He starts the engine when the alarm on his watch hits seven p.m. I head towards the passenger seat but he accelerates and I fall down. I swear under my breath and attempt to make it to the front again. Once again Tom speeds up and I lose my balance.

'Christ Tom, what is wrong with you?' I shout. I think I hear him snigger. Knowing that I am not welcome, I stay in the back. The snow comes down hard but this doesn't stop Tom's erratic driving, speeding up and then slowing down. I try to look at my compass for some idea where we are heading. North-west, towards the coast, but it is too dark to see the map.

I think of how stupid the situation is and holding on tightly, make my way to the passenger seat. Tom speeds up but I manage to hold on. Sitting next to him, I search his face for a clue.

'What's going on?'

His fingers tighten round the steering wheel.

'Where are we going?' I ask gently.

'Stay in the fuckin' back,' he spits out at me.

'No.' I can't believe his mood but can't think of anything to say or do to calm him down. So I sit there, hoping he'll come to his senses.

He applies the brakes and the camper skids across the road. We stop abruptly. We both have the wind knocked out of us. As we catch our breath, I realise that he won't drive any further while I am in the front. I undo my seatbelt and return to my sleeping bag.

I wake up as Tom slams the door behind him. It is sometime in the early hours. I try to go back to sleep but as the minutes add up I begin to feel uneasy. I check the clock on the dashboard. An hour passes and I put my coat and boots on. Damn Tom, what's he playing at. I wait another twenty minutes before I go to the door and shout. My voice sounds eerie as it whistles through the trees. There is no other sound. It has snowed heavily and Tom's footsteps are clearly imprinted heading towards the trees. I shout again, 'Tom, are you OK?'

Putting my hat and gloves on, I suck in my breath and follow Tom's footprints. The moon reflecting on the snow lights his trail into the woods. The snow becomes thinner on the ground as the trees become denser and looking down I see that his footprints have stopped. I kneel and inspect the ground closely. There are definitely no more. I turn, expecting him to jump from behind a tree.

I swear in annoyance as I realise that he has probably backtracked to trick me. Turning back in the direction I came, I hear a chugging sound. I run through the woods keeping an eye on the footprints, but the sound is fading. I keep on, but my legs are wet from the snow and feel like water filled balloons. I can't breathe and my chest is so tight. I stumble out through the first few trees to where the footprints started, to where the camper was. My map and Walkman lie in the place where it was parked. So does the present I was going to give Tom. Its gaudy paper wet and crushed in the snow. It was a novelty mug, now a flat package of broken pottery. As I wonder what to do, a police car races past, its siren blaring. I pick up my belongings and follow it up the road.

Marie Dobson
The Taste of Friday

Loose words skitter on her tongue; they are bothering her. She tries to lick them up into some kind of sense, but she can't. She hasn't tasted a word for days, only thick soupy food and the odd cigarette. She's sure they'd have been tasteless words anyway.

People once put words into her mouth. They strung them between her teeth like won't-get-lost mittens. Small washing lines of 'Yes please's and 'Excuse me's, not yet ironed and smelling of someone else's soap powder.

She has learnt that washing lines are personal. She chooses to talk beach towels and sharp suits now. She doesn't 'Yes please' and she pushes past people in the street. But now and then, when she's alone, she wonders if she ever did lose her mittens.

Friday's work-finished-words don't sponge up the after work drinks today. The flimsy pieces of all-the-same-week stay the same dry size as she listens to vodka and lime and to sweet milky cocktails, staying totally sober. The other sharp-suits have mouths stale with alcohol, swollen with drunken banter and cheap chat-up lines. She walks backwards, watches them chewing on fat opinions; opinions non-existent before half-past five. Her glasses get emptied too, but this evening everything is diluted, her drinks are as bland as her words.

Someone lights her cigarette for her. For a moment her words are

The Taste of Friday

sucked inside her with smoke. Because the someone smiles she almost believes that she caught the fleeting taste of a 'thank you' in the inhalation, but that doesn't sound like her any more.

'Bad for you, you know. Course you know. Great though, eh?' She looks up from where the smile had put her, and nods. The woman with the lighter has a colourless face, and she notices her mottled yellowed fingers hold her cigarette to her lips as if it's the finest tobacco, to be savoured. It's a roll-up, and she wonders if it's only tobacco. She could do with some of that; a taste of violation to even her out. She sucks a sizzle from her Silk Cut, watching. 'On your own? Where's the party spirit on a Friday night?' She shrugs, knocking back a watery vodka, tiny shards of ice catching her throat. Strangers always want to talk. She scrapes her chair on the tiles getting up. 'Mine's a Guinness, love.' She picks up her empty glass and the woman's scummy pint pot, and goes to the bar. Don't get on the wrong side of people you don't know.

The woman rolls a joint. Not out of sight of the bar, or the other drinkers, or the pack of sharp-suits on a nearby table.

She has never tasted drugs. She has tasted swear words and hard gristled chunks of anger. She doesn't complain, recording every twist and curl, her peripheral vision working overtime. She thinks she sees a sharp-suit glance over, but he is only watching for the teenage barmaid coming round again. Her nose is alive with a sweet sickly smell new to her, her eyes fascinated. 'Don't usually, you understand. Only cause I can't afford it!' The woman throws laughter over her shoulder for good luck and lights up. She sips silently on a double vodka, pass it to me, pass it to me — wordless. This is a new enthusiasm. The woman nips the paper between dry crumpled lips, her eyes closed. She is murmuring. She exhales, slow smoke hovering. 'Here,' she says, holding it out over the table. She takes it, locking eyes with the woman, hoping she looks in control, experienced. She doesn't know where this will take her, but the possibility of it taking her down makes it even more appealing. She hesitates — this isn't what sharp-suits do — and takes a draw.

She craves sweetness. She is whisky and gingered — in here they serve pieces of it, crystallised, on sticks. They slump against the side of each glass like miniature kebabs, dripping. She counts five, but now and again they melt together into one great sugary chunk and she wishes she had taste for more than slop.

They have rung bells at the bar and shouted over the heads of insistent punters. Another whisky kebab is stamped on the table in front of her, or is it two? The yellowy hand it came from offers muffled words but she just can't listen. She surveys the bar through fog. No-one is going home tonight.

People are playing pool, playing darts, playing away. Men with other men's pool cues and women with other wives' men. Those not in suits are in sparkle. She watches fifty-year-old chests in elasticated tinsel being watched by sixty-year-old men wishing they were still elastic enough to try them out. She pictures endless washing lines twinkling — please, please, please. She drinks her whisky.

One o'clock. The building twitches. Suits are leaving through the back door. They weave out like a badly-typed sentence. Some of the keys keep sticking. She is taken by the elbow and she imagines the tinsel-chests watching, envious, as she is smudged into darkness. She realises, when she tastes the fresh air, that her words have stopped skittering.

Patrick Murphy

Gulf Crisis

I injected a girl in the neck once.
Will you give us a hit she said in between
chasing cars round the red light district
where we both lived and moved and had our being.
She undid her belt, placed one end through the other
to form a noose and dropped it over her head
like she was lowering her halo. She pulled tight
There she said scratching her forefinger
gently along a vein.

There's a petrol shortage I said
It's to do with this Gulf crisis.
Cars are queuing round the block
Middle England's gone crazy
for petrol.

The pumps are the busiest I've seen them
said the the guy in the all night garage.

My business would go to pot if there was no petrol
No petrol means no kerb crawlers
means no more hand jobs for five pouns
or blow jobs for ten or unprotected sex
for a score.
Yes, that Saddam's lost the plot I said
as I pumped her full of fluid.

Caron Henderson
Alice In Sunderland
from a novel in progress

Chapter Thirteen

The room is long, a bar at one end and a small stage at the other. Tables and chairs clutter the middle. Already, there's a buzz of people and the air's weighty with cigarette smoke and perfume. Lights dance over us from the glitterball hanging over the empty dance floor.

What am I doing here? I have this urge to turn around and leave but Julie grabs my arm and pulls me towards the bar.

'Reet, what do yer want?' She produces a tiny purse from a tint bag that dangles down from her neck and into her cleavage.

'Ermm I'll have a lager please.'

'Lager! Why no! What with the day you've had? No, I know exactly what you need. You're having a cocktail.'

'But...'

'But nothing. Where's that barmaid?' Julie takes a ten-pound note from the purse and starts waving it above her head. 'Howay Doreen, a girl could die of thirst waiting for you!'

'Hold yer horses. I've only got one pair a hands.' A tired looking woman lumbers from the far end of the bar. 'The usual, Julie?'

'Na, we'll have two Slammers to start with.'

'I'll sort these, Doreen.' A bloke with a neat white shirt and crisp moustache nudges her to one side. 'You'd better go and check the gents.

Someone said it's blocked up again.' Then he turns to Julie, all teeth and gum. 'Two Slammers was it, Julie?'

'Aye, Reg.'

He busies with glasses and bottles. 'Who's your friend?' He asks looking at me.

'This is Ali.'

'Pleased to meet you, Ali.' He puts out a hand. I look at it and put mine out. Then he lifts my hand to his lips and kisses it. Julie snorts. His lips are hot, moist. When he lets go, I wipe my hand on the back of my jeans after he returns to the drinks.

'There you go, two Slammer Specials for two lovely young ladies.'

'Ta, Reg.' Julie starts to hand him the money but with a quick glance over his shoulder, he waves it away. 'No darlin', these are on me.' Then he winks. I feel sick.

'Howay, let's grab that table.' Julie points, grabs the drinks and is off. I follow her, still rubbing the back of my hand. Julie pulls out a chair and sits. She sees my face and laughs. 'Don't mind Reg. He's like that with all the new faces. He's harmless. Anyway, he wouldn't dare do anything with Doreen about. She'd kill him. Come on now, drink up. Down in one.' She lifts the glass to her lips and glugs. 'God, that hit the spot!'

I look at my glass. 'I'm not sure I should be doing this.'

'Go on. It's nice, really.'

'No, I don't mean the drink. I just think it might have been a mistake to come out.'

'Oh Ali, don't say that. You need a break, you canna just sit in the house feeling bad. It's not like you're doing wrong against Darren's memory. This'll take you're mind off it.'

'Will it?'

'Aye, after a few of those you won't remember a thing. Ha!' Then she looks at me. 'Look, at least stop for a while, if you're still feeling crap then you can always go home later. Yeah?'

'I suppose...'

'Now get that drink down your neck!'

I look suspiciously at my glass. 'What's in it?'

'Best not to ask. Gan on!'

I lift the glass and sniff. Could be tequila or vodka or...I take a sip.

'That's no good, man. Down in one.' Julie pushes my elbow.

So, I swallow it in one gulp. The liquid scorches as it passes down my throat and I cough and choke. Julie pounds my back. 'Great. I'll get us some more.' I try to say that I don't want another but I seem to have lost the use of my tongue. When my eyes stop watering, Julie has returned with two more drinks. She grins at me as she sits down. 'There you go. Put hair on your chest that will!' She laughs, giving me a great view of her fillings. 'Fuck, I'm gagging for a tab. You got any?'

I shake my head.

'Reet, I'll have to cadge some off Reg then. Back in a tick.'

I watch as she totters to the bar on her impossibly high heels. She and Reg chat for a while. I think they're talking about me 'cause Reg stares over Julie's shoulder and when he sees me clock him, looks away. The bar is getting busy, middle-aged couples, groups of lads in fluorescent shirts. Reg has to leave Julie and help Doreen serve. I take a sip of my drink and wince. Julie returns with a packet of Embassy King-size and two more drinks.

'You all right?' She straddles the chair, tricky in such a tight skirt but she manages it. 'Whey, you've not finished that one yet! Life down South turned you soft?' She lifts her glass and swallows in one. As if to prove a point, I do the same. Funny, it doesn't seem so bad this time. Julie tugs a cigarette from the packet, slips it between lipsticked lips. 'You want one?'

'No, thanks.'

'Fuck it, no lighter.' She turns to a table of fat, bald men about six feet away from us and yells, 'Hey Macca, gis a light.'

One of the men chucks a lighter across to her with a laugh. 'Keep it Julie, or you'll not stop bothering us all night!'

Julie lights her cigarette and shouts back, 'That'll make a change. Normally, you're the one bothering me. What's the matter? The missus coming in tonight?' She laughs.

The blokes all snigger but when Julie turns back to me, smoke curling, she says, 'Aren't men wankers?' Then we start laughing until everyone starts looking and my face is damp with tears.

'Oh, stop. I'm going to piss mysell!' Julie snorts. Then we both lift our glasses and down them in one. 'Now, look, we're out of drink.'

'I'll get these.' I stand, searching inside my jeans pocket for some money.

'Na, my treat.' Julie pulls me down and stands up.

'But...' She's gone. Where does she get all this money? Then I remember the brand new clothes I'd spotted in her wardrobe this afternoon. She said that she'd won it gambling. I'm mulling this over when I think of another thing that's been bothering me. Darren's friends calling at her house. What has she got in common with a bunch of eight-year olds? That crap she said about them running errands for her! A burst of noise from the stage distracts me. A man in a sparkly suit has been setting up equipment and is testing the microphone. 'One two. One two.' There is a burst of feedback and everyone flinches. 'Sorry about that ladies and gentlemen. My name's Tony and I'm your DJ and karaoke host for the evening. If you have any requests...'

'Aye, I've got one...fuck off, you ponce.' One of the bald blokes bellows and all of his mates crack up.

'Thank you. Any requests for music or if you want to put your name down for karaoke please let me know.' Tony seems unflustered, must get that kind of stick all the time.

'Hey! Do you fancy that?' Julie is back, glasses in hand. Great, I love karaoke me. Let's get our names down quick. I always like doing Madonna stuff best. She's ace, isn't she?'

'Julie, I wanted to ask you about this afternoon.'

But she is standing, peering at the stage. 'I'd better get mysell up there afore that bitch Linda gets her name down. She's always hoggin' the soddin' mike.' Then she turns frowning back to me. 'What'd yer say, Ali?'

'Darren's friends? I wanted to...' My voice disappears under a burst of sound as Disco Tony starts spinning his discs.

'I'll just be a minute. You want me to put your name down?' Julie leans in, shouts into my ear.

I shake my head. She's off, squeezing past tables, chatting to people as she passes on the way to Disco Tony. I lift my glass to take a drink but am surprised to see it empty. Can't remember drinking it. Julie's glass is empty too. I suppose I'd better get us some more. It's a bit of a struggle to get to the bar. The place is pretty crowded, all the tables are now taken and also my legs seem to have gone a bit wobbly. Probably that running this afternoon. I'm just about at the bar when a group of lads, well, blokes really, catch my attention. They are gathered at the bar end, pints in hands, talking loudly and laughing. I don't know why I'm staring but they look kind of familiar. I can't seem to focus properly, must be the light. One of them clocks me and nudges the one next to him, then they're all looking. I look away.

'Yes, darlin'. What can I get you?' Reg asks.

'Oh, er...two of them Slammer things, please.'

'Coming right up.'

I fumble in my pocket for the money.

'Ali? It is you isn't it?' A deep voice just behind me.

I turn and it's one of the blokes from the end of the bar.

'It is! Christ, it must be...what? Eight, no, nine years since I last saw you? How are you?' Then he looks at me all smiles and I'm searching his face, trying to get my stupid brain together to come up with who-the-fuck this bloke with a goatee is. Then it hits me. John. John Dougan. Suddenly, I go all hot then cold.

'You all right?' He asks.

I try to pull myself together, but my legs feel weird and my stomach has flipped. 'Yeah, fine. Thanks.' I mumble.

'It was Kenny that spotted you. You remember Ken? Always getting into bother at school. Not like us, eh?' He laughs. I remember his laugh, rich and deep.

'John. Of course.' I try to smile but my face feels tight, frozen.

'In the flesh! More of it than I'd like an' all.' He pats his belly with red-knuckled hands. I recall a wash-board stomach, hands that stroked my...

'That's three pounds fifty, darlin'.' Reg, with my drinks.

I flush, turn to him. Hand him a fiver.

'So what brings you here? I thought you lived in London? Visiting the family, eh?' Then his face falls. 'God, sorry, Ali. I heard about your brother. It just slipped my mind when I saw you there. I'm so sorry.'

I wave a hand at him. 'Don't worry about it.'

We stand in uncomfortable silence or as silent as you can get in the middle of a busy club.

John speaks first. 'You look well. Haven't changed a bit.'

'Thanks.' I mutter, 'You look...the same too.'

'Get away with you. I must be about four stone heavier.' He pats his belly again. 'That's what married life does to you. You got any bairns? Me and the missus, you must remember Andrea, have got three now and another on the way.' He takes a swig of beer. I watch his Adam's apple bob as he swallows.

'I'd better take these back. Julie'll be wondering where I've got to.' I pick up the drinks.

'Oh, right. It's been great to see you, Ali. Catching up and that.'

'Yeah. Bye.' My hands shake as I make my way back to the table. I want to look around at him but I know he's still watching me. I can almost feel his eyes on my back.

'Ace. You've got us some more drinks. God, I had to have this reet barney with that old cow,' Julie turns and points at a woman standing at the bar, 'cause she tried to nick our table. Fucking cheek of some people! Hey! Was that Johnny Dougan you was talking to? Can you remember at school, how everyone fancied him? He was so lush. Not that you can tell now like. Had to marry that Andrea. She was in the year below us. He knocked her up and her Da caused such a scene, they had to wed. I always fancied him. Did you?'

'Not really.' I can almost taste the memory. Harsh kisses moving from my lips to my neck. Me pushing him away in case he left a mark.

'Just as well 'cause we'd never have stood a chance with him. He was courting that Denise for years and she'd knack anyone who even looked at him. Still he must had gone behind her back with Andrea. I bet she wasn't the first.'

Pulling me down onto the warm, damp grass. Whispering love. Fumbling with my clothes. Saying he would be careful. Looking over his shoulder in case anyone should spy us.

'You all right? Only you've gone a funny colour.' Julie's words make me jump.

'Err...I'm fine. I just need to go to the toilet.'

'You're not going to puke, are you?'

'No. Where's the toilet?'

'Just through those doors then turn left. You want me to come with you?'

'No. I'll be fine. Thanks.'

'Howay! There's people pissed themsell out here!' The shouting is followed by a pounding on the cubicle door. I'd been sitting, trying to stop my head from spinning and to get my thoughts straight. With a sigh, I pull up my knickers and jeans. I try to flush the toilet but it just gurgles sadly at me. As I open the door, a woman in a lycra sundress shoves me out of the way and vomits into the toilet bowl. Another woman follows her and pats her on the back. 'Get it all up, pet. Soon as you're done we can get down the town clubbin'.'

I head back to the bar. At the door, I hesitate. Should I just call it a night? I don't want to bump into John again. But what about Julie? Sighing, I pull open the door. Julie has company at our table. A bloke wearing a stripy blazer and holding a tray is standing next to her. Julie sees me and waves.

'I thought you might feel better with some food in your belly. So I got you some crab sticks.' She waves them under my nose.

I push them away. 'No thanks but I don't eat fish.'

'Oh. Want some whelks then?' She offers me a tub and stick. I shake my head. 'You feeling better then? 'Cause I got you something else to drink in case those Slammers didn't agree with you. Double vodka and tonic.'

I see John at the bar. He glances my way. I feel this sudden urge for a strong drink. 'Cheers!' I lift up my glass and drink it down.

'Aye, cheers.' Julie downs her drink. 'Not long till the karaoke starts. Where the fuck are Yvonne and Lynn?'

'Who?'

'You know, me so-called mates. Them that was supposed to be here half a fuckin' hour ago!' Julie scans the room.

'Julie, you never answered me properly about Darren's mates.'

'What about them?' She's still looking around.

'It's been on my mind, what you said about them going to the shops for you. You don't really expect me to believe that?'

She turns to me with flashing eyes. 'You calling me a liar?'

'No. That's not what I meant.'

'Well, that's what it sounds like!'

I take a deep breath. 'It just seems strange that...'

'There they are!' Julie jumps up, waving her arms in the air. 'Yoohoo! Over here.'

I give up and let myself be smothered in a cloud of perfume and lipstick kisses from Yvonne and Lynn who are very pissed and treat me like I'm their long-lost mate.

The night spirals from then on. I never seem to be without a drink. We are dancing and singing and dancing and drinking. Then it all gets a bit blurry. I'm looking for Julie 'cause her name has been called to sing 'Like a Virgin'. I stagger towards the toilet, see if she's there. But she's not so I start to head back to the bar. Loud voices from the end of the corridor. I peer around a corner. Julie and a chunky no-neck bloke. Can't hear what they are saying. Then they disappear out a side door. I tag along. The door opens onto the carpark. It's very dark. The only light comes from a street light over the other side of the road. There are just two cars parked. Julie and bloke sit in one of them. I see them only when he lights a cigarette. In the flare from the match, it looks like they're arguing. Then the car door slams. Julie marches across the car park. She sees me.

'Ali! What you doin' here?'

Behind her, the car engine roars into life. We are lit up like startled deer in the headlights. Gravel spurts as the car screams forward.

'Julie! Watch out!' I drag her out of the way as the car hurtles towards us. We land in a tangle as it shoots past and onto the road.

Adam Fish

Travel

Cracking
       The gates of the moon
gum.
    The acrobat monster
The gates of the surgery.
                              Half-girl cut
Crazy-paved drive. Talk on mobiles. The girl
                Cracking mask
who looks just like Michelle.

    to be cut up

The acrobat's mask. The half-cut
          The acrobat's outside
                The monster looks just like Michelle
moon. The monster
       The surgery moon
is
      crazy-paved girl
out-side.

                          Outside:
                    Talk of gum.

                    Gates cracking.

        The acrobat's crazy-paved moon.

              The monster surgery.

                The girl half-cut.

                Michelle just looks.

tobecutuptobecutuptobecutuptobecutuptobecutupto

City of Seahorses

An arthritic car pulls up outside.
It sneezes its greeting. I climb in the back.
The driver changes the radio
from news to Gorecki to Steps.

I light up a
cigarette. Drunks
stagger past us, wallets bruised.
A man in a purple shirt and a woman
in a black dress caress in a doorway.
She has a bottle of Hooch by her waist
and they fuck without spilling a drop.

A girl in a mini-skirt's shouting at
a boy with a shaved head and trainers
too clean to have ever been ran in.
There's tears in her eyes but he throws up his hands,
gold-ringed, shouts back and walks away.

Katherine Zeserson
The Mother's Face
from a novel in progress

Manhattan, early August 1991
Frances comments

We went to Manhattan. I hated the journey to the city. I hated the way the lush landscape gradually decayed into broken-down concrete and car-crushing plants. I defiantly wore white, notwithstanding the likelihood of greasy smears under my arms. Rosa chain-smoked all the way.

We listened to Suzanne Vega singing about a girl called Luka. Bizarre name. I am interested in names and naming, in the potency of language as a determinant of identity; as a confirmer of existence. I like that.

Rosa, of course, was named after Rosa Luxemburg, and her middle name is Dolores, after Dolores Ibirere. La Pasionaria. Julian was named after the hero of Stendhal's Red and Black, and his middle name is Reid after John 'Ten Days that Shook the World' Reid. What a burden of responsibility. My own name is much more straightforward. Frances was my paternal grandmother, Connolly is my mother's surname, and Moore is a quiet but distinguished kind of tag — young students eager to please with their assiduity offer me apples, and want to know if I met Bertrand Russell as a child. My father was not a philosopher, in defiance of family trend, nor even an academic, but then they say these things often skip generations.

I tried a conversation with Rosa about names as we drove along and instantly regretted it, because she started on about the annihilation of identity experienced by immigrants at Ellis Island, and how few kept the names they'd arrived with because the immigration officers couldn't be bothered to spell them properly, or hear them properly, or perhaps took some sadistic pleasure in robbing people of their patrimony, although it seemed to me if their greatest loss after the rigours of the journey and the trauma of departure was simply the spelling of their surnames, then I thought they'd probably done rather well. It was neither a productive nor an amiable conversation.

I was sick of it. Self-indulgent, retrogressive egotistical nonsense. All this carrying on as if the Jews held a monopoly on suffering. I am half-Irish, but do I keep on about Cromwell or the potato famine? No. I think it's more interesting to go forward, to construct yourself from what is around you right here and right now and be free of all that. I see history differently, from the philosophical perspective. The study of history tells us about historians, not about ourselves. Accepting a linear, causal theory of personality development across generations leads the clear thinker into fatalism. I don't accept that. I am, in that conflict, an Idealist.

We'd been building up over this for about two months, ever since Rosa had gone on a visit to Lithuania with Hy. They had been away for two weeks, and come back with six notebooks full of commentary, which she was now working over, re-writing adding to, illustrating with clippings and photocopies from old books and newspapers. First thing in the morning, she reached for her notebook. I fell asleep at night to the sound of her slithering pen. (She always used an old Schaeffer given to her by Julian.) I sometimes imagined jumping up and down on the end of the bed shouting 'see me! I exist! I am your lover! I am very nice and interesting too!' She would look up, smile vaguely, and go back to the notebook.

It was disturbing my sleep. I'd watch her in repose, trying to make her remember me. I felt like a spy. I didn't like being jilted by ghosts, by dreams, by illusions. It made me doubt my own corporeality.

We arrived at Julian's clammy and out of sorts, and found him pale.

'Hi you guys. You look great. Living in the country suits you.'

His voice was gravelly and hollow.

'Come on, let's have a drink.'

We sat on his terrace, breathing in the oily city air, and reported on the state of the garden, the plumbing, the neighbours. I let Rosa and Julian do the talking.

I had met Julian first, at a music festival in Massachusetts. He was there singing with his choir, and I was being a tourist, or maybe an anthropologist, trying to understand the culture of the place. I'd only been in the States about three months, and had spent most of my time getting to grips with my work, psycholinguistics research, and learning the inadaquacies of American grammar. I was determined to be urbane and comfortable about moving three thousand miles, but actually I was feeling extremely wrong-footed.

I met Rosa right here on his terrace at the end of that summer, as the evenings were growing chill. He set the meeting up, unashamedly matchmaking and within half an hour I was hooked. She fascinated me. She was angry. She was beside herself, sparking with rage about something or other; I can't remember any of the details now, I don't think I listened to a word she said, just the rich musical voice she spoke in, and I couldn't take my eyes off her face. Julian kept us supplied with gin and tonic, and when it grew too cold to sit out, the three of us went and ate Brazilian food and danced, wildly, till three a.m., my first introduction to New York night-life. I didn't know myself, sweating and swaying, laughing and shouting over the band, being American — I liked it. Saying goodbye, she kissed both my cheeks and my stomach turned over. I knew I was lost.

Watching them on the terrace almost a year later, I marvelled at the puzzling qualities of time, how it elongates and contracts depending on how interesting has been its passage. Rosa's laugh brought me back.

'Earth to Frances, Earth to Frances, where are you?'

'Sorry. Daydreaming. Thinking about time.'

She reached over and laid her hand upon my head, recently shaved, not quite skinhead, just a quarter inch cut.

'Suedehead. I love the feel of this. Feel it Julian, it's gorgeous.'

He stroked my head.

'Wonder what Ida will make of you?'

'Don't suppose she'll be able to make anything of me as we'll not be meeting.'

'Actually I was going to talk to you about that.'

Rosa sounded a little embarrassed.

'I've agreed to help Ida organise a family dinner at the end of the month. We really wanted to get everyone together, it's ...we've never done that before, and I guess I figured you'd come with me.'

I looked at her. I said nothing.

'They know who you are, I mean it's not like we'd have to pretend or anything.'

'I've told you. I don't want to meet your family.'

'Oh come on Fran, don't be so rigid. It's really important to me.'

I hated it when she called me Fran. She always said it in a little girl voice, the kind people use to babies and animals.

I said nothing.

The atmosphere was shot. Julian coughed and ran his fingers through his hair. Rosa crossed her arms and frowned.

'Why do you have to be so fucking prickly? What's so hard about meeting our family?'

'It doesn't matter. Just leave it.'

She turned away from me and leaned on the terrace wall. I felt mean, but hard. I would not be treated like a pet, displayed on a lead, well-groomed. I would not be half of a couple, either, and I would not be sucked into self-indulgent displays of emotion. I continued to sip my drink. I would not be the next to speak.

I was always a great believer in silence. That's why I hated being aroused to passionate anger. The words tumbled out before I could organise them. Rosa thought out loud. I could love to watch her face seeking meaning from the sound of her voice, and I could also be driven mad by it. I was determined, however, to keep the relationship going, if only for its anthropological value.

That's a lie, actually. I wanted to keep the relationship going because I'd never really managed to sustain one before, and I was starting to feel like a failure. Her very difference and strangeness allowed a certain latitude between us, a tolerance that counted for a lot. And she was beautiful, and had a boundless energy, and I was obsessed with her.

Matthew Pacey
A Good Reputation

Down behind the chippy the waggers would always wait for us at dinnertimes. Sitting on the empty market stall with greasy fingers drinking cherry Coke. It seemed like you knew who you were. We'd chat up the younger girls from the years below us. They loved to be seen with fifth-formers. They thought it made them look so cool and mature, and it gave them something to scrawl over their textbooks during the afternoon lessons.

    Louise 4 Denny.

    Jo-Jo 4 Bainesy.

    Nicky is a wanker.

    We loved it too, though of course, we'd never admit it.

    Friday nights it was different down there, more poisonous. Greasy fingers belonged to bigger hands. You'd smoke out of cans and drink litre bottles 'til your eyes went red. If you puked it didn't matter, so long as you carried on drinking. That way people would think you were hard, or that you didn't give a shit. Either way, it meant that you wouldn't get messed with.

    It was always good to have someone like Malley down there on a Friday night. Malley was reputable. He kept us safe. He taught us to stand and take the punch, even when we knew we couldn't win the fight.

    'Cause that's how you get respect,' he said. 'That's how you earn yourself a reputation.'

    Malley was Nicky's older brother and cock-of-the-hill. Nobody messed with him on this side of town. He hated Nicky like you hate a nosebleed, but watched over him anyway. Nicky was such a scrawny little shit. Half the size we were. He couldn't have punched his way through paper but because of his older brother, he got away with daylight robbery. He'd play up to whoever he liked. Fella's two and three times harder than him sometimes and they wouldn't say jip 'cause they knew that if they did, they'd have Malley to answer to. It used to make me mad, the way Nicky went on. But I never said anything, he was a mate after all.

Malley had two rules, which he lived by. The first one was that he never hit girls. The second was that whatever he was faced with, he would always consider his reputation above all other things.

'In this town,' he used to say to us, 'a reputation's the soundest weapon you can carry. You don't need to be hard, or a good fighter. If you've got reputation, nobody'll mess with you.'

He taught us that it was nothing to do with how hard you hit, more to do with the way you act, the way you hold yourself. In certain situations, you didn't even need to fight.

'For example,' he said, 'supposing you're out on a Friday night and some make-out fuckwit starts playing the hard man. Some pissed-up low-life gimp who reckons he can get the better of you. What do you do? You're not gonna earn any respect by getting involved with this creep. Everyone knows you can leather him anyway. So walk away. It's simple as that. If the shitbag throws a punch at you, you have to take it. You have to act like this is below you. Because that's how people know not to mess. When they see you laughing at some skinny little niner because he just gave you his best punch to the face, it shows them that you don't need to prove yourself. You're there already.'

Barry Bubble was Malley's best mate. One was rarely seen without the other. Barry Bubble was soft as shite and thick as a pig. It was almost as if Malley used him to strengthen his own reputation. Like Nicky, Barry was someone Malley could protect.

'If you hang around with a group of hard lads all the time, eventually people'll start to ask why,' Malley's theory went. 'It doesn't take them long to figure out that it's because you're a soft shit yourself. Look at all those Valley boys for Christ's sake, wandering around in gangs, carrying flick-knives in their pocket. Soft shites the lot of them. It stands to reason.'

Like Nicky, Barry Bubble was pretty much a free agent on the hill. He did what he liked and got away with it. Every other night you'd see him down the Tut'n'Shive, pissed out his skull and feeling up some lassie five or six years the younger than him. She'd normally be throwing a fit, screaming and slapping him in the face and the like. 'You see Barry Bubble wasn't just as soft and thick as a pig, he was as ugly as one too. But the lads would always stand off. It didn't matter whose girl it was Barry was fondling, they'd never lay a finger on him. 'Cause they knew who Barry's best mate was.'

Whenever anyone asked Malley to his face why he liked Barry, he'd say straight out.

'I don't. He's a fuckwit!'

And this was pretty much what he thought about his brother too. But still, nobody was willing to take the chance, and for years, Nicky and Barry Bubble got away with blue murder on the hill.

In the summer we used to go up Castle Hill and drink Stella and watch the shiny, clean girls walking home to mummy's and daddy's at Oaktrees, on the other side of the canal. Castle Hill was a good spot. You could see the whole town from up there and watch the sun go down over the water. If it was raining you could go under the Canal Bridge, and smoke a can without fear of being disturbed by the rozzers. It stunk of piss down there, and the walls were all covered with shit saying who was with who and who they'd been with before that. Sometimes the girls'd leave a phone number and you'd phone it up just for a laugh. Nicky used to do that all the time and talk real dirty. One time we caught him doing it and pulling his pud at the same time. He was a dirty bastard was Nicky.

Then one summer we went down there and found the place all full of sniffers. About ten of them. All sat around in their little groups, sniggering into their plastic bags. Everyone hated the sniffers. They drifted around the town like a bad smell.

'What are you lot doing here?' Bainesy asked them.

'Dennis turfed us out the sub-station.'

'Well you can't stay here.' Nicky said.

'What?'

'I said you can't stay here. This is our bridge.'

'Yeah, what you gonna do Nicky?' Tammy Flinton chirped up. 'Get big brother on to us?'

Tammy looked like shit. She'd been sniffing for years. Injecting too.

She'd do anything for a ten bag of smack, and I mean anything! She was a proper dirty cow. She stood up and walked over to Nicky.

'You think you're so fucking hard Nicky. Just 'cause of your big brother. That's all it is. You couldn't beat up a lass like me even if you wanted to.'

'Shut up you whore.'

Tammy pushed Nicky towards the canal.

'Don't call me a whore you little shit. Come on, hit me if you're so hard.'

So Nicky leaned back and threw a fist at Tammy's face. She screamed and jerked her head back but didn't go down. She just stood there, her nose bleeding and her eyes red raw from all the glue she'd sniffed. We just stood there too, and watched as she picked Nicky up like a loose pebble, and slung him into the canal. Then she burst out laughing.

Nicky stood in the water, so shocked he couldn't move, with all the shit from the canal hanging off him.

'Where's big brother now Nicky boy?' she screeched.

'You fucking whore,' Nicky shouted, 'I'm gonna get you for this. I'm gonna get all your druggie scum friends as well. Dirty shits.'

He was furious. He climbed out the canal and took off his shirt. He squeezed it out on the path, then threw it at the sniffers sat on the bank. Tammy was laughing her tits off. The rest of the sniffers were just sitting there, quietly vacant.

They knew that it wasn't going to be Tammy who suffered for this one.

As we walked home Nicky was in such a foul temper that he would hardly even talk to us. He said that we'd betrayed him, by not taking his side against Tammy. He called us pussies.

'But we could hardly have hit the bitch could we?' Bainesy said.

'Why not?' said Nicky.

'Well, because she's a bitch isn't she? You know what you're brother always says about hitting lassies Nicky.'

'You all make me sick,' Nicky snarled at us. 'The way you all suck up to my brother so much. You act like he's some kind of God. Well he's not. He's nothing but a soft piece of shit.'

He stormed off in a huff. When he'd gone we all sat on the wall, and laughed our tits off.

Nicky wagged off school all week. All the rest of us talked about was who the unlucky victim was likely to be. Malley had to do something. He couldn't let Tammy Flinton humiliate his little brother without taking it out on someone. He had a reputation to think about. But he would never hit Tammy, it was against his rules. And to start on the sniffers would do his reputation more harm than good. Soft druggie shites like that were surely beneath him. So who was it going to be?

When Friday night came we all got down the market stalls well early. We took a litre bottle of cider each and made sure that we got front row seats for the show. As the night drew on, a fair old crowd turned up. Word spreads quickly in a small town like this one and there was talk that the Valley Boys might have heard, and may well decide to poke their ugly noses in. Then we'd have had a real night on our hands. But the Valley Boys never turned up, and neither did Malley.

It wasn't until the next day that we heard that Barry Bubble was in hospital. Apparently, him and Malley had been out on the raz the night before. People were saying that they'd seen them together in the Tut'n'Shive. Malley was buying all the drinks and Barry Bubble was getting himself into a right old state. Later in the night, the two of them went down the Unicorn, which is a real busy, townie kind of place. You have to queue up to get in there, and apparently, whilst in the queue, Barry Bubble got up to his usual tricks with some Valley Girl who was stood in front. She was with some Valley Boys, and they asked Malley (quite politely by all accounts) to pull Barry off.

Malley didn't just pull Barry off, he burst the Bubble for good. Beat seven shades of shit out of him, in front of everyone. It was a totally unprovoked attack, so the people who saw it said. Malley was going at his best mate like a rabid dog to a leg. Eventually the police had to pull him off.

Barry Bubble was hospitalised for ten days. He had a broken nose, a broken cheekbone, and three fractured ribs. Malley was detained by the rozzers. It wasn't until the trial that we learned why Malley had attacked his best mate in this way. Allegedly, Barry Bubble was a bit of a speed-king and had been supplying some top-grade, out of town shit to Tammy Flinton in exchange for whatever he could get. Malley had known about it, he was probably even involved in it. Who knows? He'd certainly had no objections until his best mate's shag decided to throw his little brother into the canal. Then he'd been forced to choose.

Malley got fourteen months for the beating he gave Barry Bubble. He got out after ten and I remember the first thing he said to us.

'A stretch in jail never did any harm to anyone's reputation.'

Gareth Rowe

Upon First Looking Into Raymond Carver

after Linda France and John Keats

Dirty Realism? Sure! This is life —
Up from the street - shovelled up with the trash.

America — the open ended land!
The sprawling cities! The wide expanses!

You wander like Boeing from coast to coast,
Leaving these perfect lines of pollution —
This mirror that shows where you're calling from.

I've wallowed on your sidewalk for weeks now,
Metaphorically —
               (I've stayed clean really).

True life in Glorious Technicolor
Brought to you in the comfort of your home —

Back here winter evenings still settle down
With steak (and a bottle of New World red).

I'd drink poison rather than face your life.

Gary Player

A Star Is Born

A place of solitude,
Mug of tea,
A Sun to read.

My my Cindy
From Brummie land
Is a well built lass.

A push, a shove,
Gravity does the rest,

And into the world
Is forced another
Joaby.

Chris Coles

Two Englynion

Sun-freckles bloom soft-brown and warm her face.
Her back is darkly sown
with constellations unknown,
scattered out, across and down.

Cerys eyes the blue crib, window shopping
on her own, belly big.
Caught in nature's game of tig.
New life kicking at a rib.

Angela Readman
Goose

'Stop jiggling Amy, for heaven's sake. I've told him a thousand times not to get your hopes up like this.'

The child is upright, careful not to crease new cotton, bobbing up and down in front of the window. She squeaks her sandals together, and dips down again.

A shape is cast across next door's fence. Dark hair. A man. Not her father. A headscarved woman with shopping bags rests on the garden wall.

'He's not coming,' says Amy's mother.

Amy's parents pass one another by, and she cannot imagine that they have ever been on the same page, like the mummy and daddy in Peter and Jane. As different as sherbert and the liquorice you dip in; Amy understands that her parents will not get back together.

'I knew this would happen. I knew it', Mum says. And when she has said it, she says it again.

Amy stares straight ahead. My dad is coming...now. No...now. For a whole sixty seconds she looks at the ground and counts, when she opens her eyes he will be here. Then he is.

'You look posh. What've you done with my daughter?'

Amy laughs.

'You're fifteen minutes late,' Mum mutters .

But it does not matter now. The child looks down at her new dress, her arms stiff at each side of fabric; hands grip the edges, pull the crisp cotton skirt to its fullest width at each side. The girl spins, shows him the back, pleased her mother didn't allow her to wear the dungarees.

'Are you ready?' he asks. From behind his back, he pulls a blue and white baseball cap, and plonks it unevenly on top of the parting the mother has struggled to untangle into a straight sleek path.

'Everyone needs a holiday hat,' he says. 'There's one here for your mum if she wants one.' He pulls a bigger baseball cap from his inside pocket and glances at the woman tying double knots on suitcase labels.

She does not look back. 'Her purse is in here, tissues, sun lotion, travel pills for the journey. Mum gave her spending money, make sure she doesn't waste it.'

He has already turned. Whistling, a bag in each hand, he loads the back of a car, whilst Amy's mother hands her a jacket, tightens the bows in her hair and slips her a sheet of paper covered in phone numbers, in case of emergency. Amy wipes her cheek where she has kissed her goodbye.

On the coach, an old lady wanders up and down in the aisles offering chunks of chocolate to all the other passengers. There is not enough, and Amy is the only person on the bus to hold out her hand for a chunk. Amy and her father swap seats when the film begins so that she can see. He has seen it before anyway, he says, and Amy is allowed to pick whatever she wants from the woman with the trolley when she squeaks past.

Sandwiches, fizzy pop, cocoa, apples, oranges, crisps, chocolate bars and hard sweets — in a huge packet — you can suck. She takes a long time over her decision. Her father does not make her eat the fruit, or remind her to eat the savoury things before the confectionary. Amy does not see why she must always save the best till last. She selects a family sized pack of the kind of sweets she can make last a long time and spreads out the fruit gems on her lap.

He fishes in his pocket for change, pays with a shaking hand. 'Egg or tuna?' He looks down carefully at the labels on the cellophane.

'Egg.'

He tosses the sandwich to Amy, who peels off the wrapper, allowing the sloppy mayonnaise mixture to leak out of the sides of the baguette onto her hands. She licks her fingers.

It is a long time on the coach. Nobody watches the movies or looks at the food-cart when it passes. Amy's father drinks from a bottle in his bag and sleeps, the corduroy seat making lines in his face. Amy presses her nose against the window. It is getting warmer.

On the ferry she collects perfume samples from a nice lady behind a counter. She flits out to the deck, watches the water making foam fans behind them.

The bus trundles through France, it does not look like Amy expected. Motorways, clouds, signs. She smudges the glass, searching factory chimneys for the Eiffel Tower. Somewhere they cross to another country. She rests her head on her father's shoulder, eyes shut until Spain.

The new dress is tea-towel crumpled, bleached by the glaring sunlight as she steps off the coach. Everything looks different in the brightness. The sides of the buildings, gravelly as the side of a matchbox glow like semi-precious stones. Amy is a blur of linen, too painful to look at. From her pocket she brings out the cap, pulls the peak down hard as they check in and follow a man to the door.

'Cool, dude', her father says, 'all you need now is shades,' and Amy knows he will buy her some. He carries her case, she carries his. It is lighter.

The apartment is in a complex surrounding a swimming pool, just five minutes walk from the beach. Amy has her own room, twin beds to share with a sister if she had one, a Fablon chest of drawers.

'Home sweet home,' her father says as he drops the bags down, and they look around.

Toilet, shower, sitting area — seats covered in brown flowers built into the window.

Amy walks over to the coffee table with a magazine on top, stares at the cover, a lady who looks familiar, and the magic foreign words she cannot read. Same letters, wrong order. She is a good reader for her age, her teacher, Miss Routledge, says but she needs to apply herself more. She applies herself to the letters on the exotic magazine, still unable to decipher them.

'Here's an ironing board. There's a cooker, and a fridge. You're the lady of the house, it's up to you to make us a Sunday dinner.' Together, they laugh.

He opens a cupboard with plates, bowls and cups in that do not match. The cupboard beside it is empty.

Amy doesn't think she can make a chicken; she has seen her mother put one in a silver pan in the oven, watched her gouge eyes from potatoes. And she can make bread and butter, at the press of a button she can make toast. She bends down, peers into the waist-height grill and looks at the dials, but the cooker here is different, swirly electric rings she has never used before. Strange sockets with just two pins.

'Were will we get food from?' Amy asks.

'There's a supermarket not far, were we can get beans and toast and stuff. Should be a kettle round here somewhere.'

Amy stands to attention when she finds the kettle and fills it from the tap.

'You're a life saver.' Her father tells her, and she grins as he adds strange tablets to the water. 'So we don't get poisoned.'

She nods, pretends to understand. It seems odd to her that it is so hot here, and you can't have anything to drink. Odd that grown-ups always want tea no matter how sunny it is.

He wavers as he switches the kettle on, flicks the switch back, changing his mind, wiping a crown of sweat with his bare arm till his skin is slick, 'Let's go scope the place out.'

By the pool there are girls in bright bikinis, parasols with *Martini* on the top, and wicker tables.

'May as well make our presence felt.' Amy's father sits by a tree growing from a pot.

A wet haired waiter waddles over, like a penguin on a biscuit advert, white shirt front, black bow tie on his chest. He returns, without speaking, places three drinks on the table and the bill face down.

'How come there's three drinks?'

'I'm bigger than you,' he says.

'Couldn't you just get one then another one?' she ask.

'You can't get the service,' Dad says. Careful grip, his hand encloses his drink; he raises it slowly to his lips. He nudges a coke with a pink umbrella over the slats. A small amount fizzes over the rim.

Amy watches cola drip a dark patch on the ground before it evaporates. Amy twiddles a cocktail stick, clown-nosed cherries, sliced lemon and a bendy straw you don't get in Littlewoods. Unreal. The drink makes her feel like she's on television; special. She cannot sit still, alternating between perching on the edge of her chair with her elbows on the table and twirling faster and faster around and around in her new dress, full-circle shadows fan round her.

Her father reclines, one hand shielding his eyes. 'Not bad,' he says, inspecting the golden liquid, holding it up to the light. 'Amy, this is important. If we ever get separated, go to reception and tell the woman you need the key to apartment 15A. OK?'

'OK.'

'What number?'

'15A.'

'Good girl.'

They walk side-by-side racing shadows, past raffia hats wilting like dandelions, striped people behind windscreens. In the crowds, Amy tap-dances on cobbles, proves what a big girl she is by keeping up. She nudges her father's elbow with her hand; she's no trouble. None at all. If she lived with him, he'd hardly know she was there.

'Must have taken a wrong turn somewhere.'

'We lost?'

'No. We've taken the scenic route, bit of a detour.'

It is exciting to be in a whole new country with him, but for a moment she is afraid. Dark doorways, a skinny cat runs in front of them. Here puss puss, here puss' whispers Amy, but it is gone. There is no one around to ask for directions.

A man sleeps in an alley, as they turn to retrace their steps.

He is awake, standing in front of them as they attempt to walk on.

Amy looks at the ground, staring at the stranger's feet. Hard yellow toenails curl into cracks between the cobbles, and she looks up. He wears long ragged trousers, and a dirty brown trench coat covered in grease stains. His eyes, dark as puddles, he speaks quietly, a slow incomprehensible slur. He holds out his hand and points to the girl. Amy is out of the sun, as his hand casts its shadow above her head.

'Sorry mate, no comprendé. English,' explains her father. Firmly, he takes the child by the shoulders, ushers her to one side and steps between her and the man.

Through the pyramid of her father's arm, Amy can see that the man holds a wine bottle in a paper bag. A piece of fishing twine hugs his waist; a Swiss army knife, a large handkerchief, a jumble of items hooked into the belt loops hang from him. A bird is tucked beneath the belt by its neck. Its down moves slightly on the breeze. Amy knows it is a Canadian goose like the one she fed in the park with Nan. A silent yellow beak dangles from the man's hip; the dead bird stares at the child with slate eye.

They walk away. Amy ponders that they have such ordinary birds in this parrot-bright place. Her father places her hand in his without saying a word. Following worn stones they find their way back. Her father is strong. He bends and gives her a piggy back through the spinning-topped people and Amy feels better. She is with her dad. Up in the sky. She wonders what her mother would say if she knew about the bags dumped at the foot of each bed, the ironed clothes getting more creased every second.

At the supermarket Amy is allowed to push the trolley. She leans forward, puts all her weight on the metal, and glides along polished floors. Her father buys tea-bags, powdered milk, biscuits, tinned beans, asks her what kind of cereal she likes.

Toilet rolls, Paracetamol, oranges, indigestion chews pastel as milkshake, two litres of cola for her.

'You have to keep taking in liquids,' he tells her, 'the sun dehydrates you. Keep your head covered, and drink as much as you can.' Before they reach the checkout he heaves four large containers of mineral water into the metal skeleton of the cart. 'The source of life,' he says, placing the tepid spring water on the conveyor. Bottles he replaces every day.

Children act like kids in the family club room. Boys run with plastic between their toes. Girls in vests enter talent contests, singing strange old-fashioned songs. A girl about Amy's age, with ringlets, wears a Barbie mini-skirt, smiling as she sings. *'You can't keep a horse in a lighthouse, nay, nay, nay.'*

Amy observes beside her father. She does not want to go to the children's room where they laugh at you, and dare each other to steal half-drunk pints from abandoned tables. She dances with her dad during the disco. *Come on Eileen.* He claps his hands, swaps places with her until they both have to sit down; he is parched.

Proud as proper parents on open-evening, she smiles when, at the end of the night, he sings on the Karaoke. He is the only dad not to sing *Only the Lonely*. Under blue lights he performs *How Deep is Your Love*, then *Theme from Shaft*. Faces, an audience bleached by spotlight, applaud. Amy mimes along, his backing singer.

'I asked your mum to come, all expenses paid, and she wouldn't,' he confides.

Bodies prop themselves up on each other to the last song.

'Mum would have sent me to bed hours ago, you're much more fun,' Amy says.

He smiles. 'It's a shame about your mum,' he says, 'I loved her, but we can't get on. She's the way she is, and I'm the way I am. I was no good.'

A lump the size of a baseball is in Amy's throat, and she gulps it down like medicine. She is not a baby, she understands. But she does not know why the feeling like the end of the summer holidays stays with her, as he puts his heavy arm round her shoulders. Slowly, they meander back to the apartment, his breath thick and ragged as he climbs the steps.

Amy wakes up. Sweat. Dark. The room is unfamiliar, no streetlight outside, no red light of the convector heater on the far wall. A heartbeat until she recalls where she is. She lies on one side, then the other, crumpling the loose sheets before she realises she has to go to the bathroom. Amy steps barefoot across the threshold from cord-carpeted scratchy warmth to smooth linoleum.

The lounge is breathing. A figure by the uncurtained window, the room is lit only by strands of stars. Her father, in his underwear, has his back to her. He fumbles with something in the shade, a lid unwinding, and tilts back his neck, the bottle glistening as he drinks. One bottle of water, then another as quickly. His head is a flip-top lid, his throat open to the current.

Amy is bloated watching him. She can almost hear his insides slosh when he edges nearer to the window. Outside, the lullaby sigh of the staff, sweeping away cigarette butts and emptying cans from last night, wiping down tables and placing down new coasters. She tip-toes back to bed.

'Amy?' his whisper from the door-post as he looks in. His daughter's eyes are squeezed tight as crossed fingers.

His breath is fire, his voice is strange. She exhales as he moves away; listens to him gulp back more liquid. Just three hours till she has to get up.

He is awake first, bright in the breezeless apartment, singing *My Way* Pavarotti style and frying mushrooms, as Amy rubs her eyes.

'The creature stirs.' He puts down the fish-slice to tickle her, making himself hunchback as he imitates her sleepy expression. 'What do you want to do today Miss Amy?'

She grins. Another day on holiday. Another day with the best Dad in the world.

Sundays at home are nothing like Sundays here. Nobody eats roast beef and Yorkshire pudding, or Dalesteak and roasties. They pick at hearty breakfasts. Bacon, sausage, eggs and giant mushrooms that look like upturned dinghys on pools of fat. Amy eats her father's tomato, gives him her fried bread, her plate is clean.

Later, they'll buy a kebab, he says, or some chips from a van by the beach. He gives her money to buy a blow-up rubber dolphin, or a Mickey Mouse beach towel from the sea-front shops, once she knows the way. She plays with the toy money in her hand.

'Meet you here, our spot's near the ice-cream van, remember?'

She nods. Moves through deckchairs, towels with patchwork people on them. All shades of red and brown. Bright red faces, naked white eyes, squint up at her, sunsets of white to pink, to apple-red. When she returns he throws empties into a carrier bag, swigs warm pop and takes her to the amusements, then a Knickerbocker Glory.

On the third day she buys three postcards with palm trees on the front and rainbow insect people playing in the cardboard sea. She scans the horizon, trying to spot where the photograph has been taken.

One for the grandmother, who had given her a small denim bag with an embroidered daisy on the front to wear around her neck with money in it. One to her best friend, Joanne Abbot. The final postcard is for her mother.

Dear Mam, Amy thinks hard. She has read other people's postcards, and is familiar with the form. Best handwriting.

Our flat is nice, and the weather is good. That is what they always put. What else?

There is a cafe round the corner with nice pancakes and good chips. Yesterday dad took me to a beach with five colour sand. Tomorrow we see tropical fish.

The last sentence slopes to one side, cramped as Amy makes each word smaller than the last. What comes next?

Wish you were here. Amy XX

She writes the words guiltily, quick. If she was here it would be different. There would be no discos, no dancing. It would be a school night all the time.

That evening, Amy rubs baby lotion into her father's scorched shoulders. He drinks, cringes when her fingers touch the flame-wrinkled skin. White blisters appear beneath the surface, air in used bubble wrap.

'How about that barbecue and firework display on the beach tonight?' he says.

'Fab!' says Amy. She tears off sheets of tracing paper from his back. He grits his teeth, and she holds a layer of cobwebby skin in front of him, almost transparent.

Amy and her father photograph manta ray, flat as pancakes. Watch a killer whale jump through a hoop. Cautiously, Amy pats its wet head, smooth and warm as a boiled egg. She does not think of the plastic bulls, and satin flags they saw as the coach pulled away. She had asked him why they weren't on it.

'It's the bullfight,' he said. 'I don't think its the sort of thing you should see.'

And she nodded.

At the barbecue a teenage girl talks about the matador as if he was a pop star, fingering the features of a souvenir man with a hat like a paper boat. Amy eavesdrops, looks over shoulders at glossy programmes. Her father queues with paper plates for pieces of fish and meat, charred on a black metal grill, promises to bring her a bit of everything.

Amy walks away from the chatter of the bullfight, she didn't want to go anyway. She walks along the sand, past the coloured lanterns, to where the sea turns black. Then blacker. It is the postcard they never took, this part of the beach, all shingles and driftwood. Deserted. Then she sees him. The crazy goose man.

He perches by a small fire surrounded by rocks, corrugated metal makes a windbreak behind him. In his hands lies a goose, larger than the one before, white feathers puffed up and floating in the evening chill. Amy watches for some time, as it makes the odd noise, an indignant honk, and the man leans towards it, strokes its breast with large earthy hands. He raises its pillow body high in the air, moves his arms in a circular motion. One, two, three times. And around.

Amy wants to see the goose. She creeps nearer, making herself small and flat in the ink of the sea wall. He must live here. Barefoot, asking for spare change from tourists. She wonders where he got the birds from. She feels like an explorer. Bravely, she creeps closer.

The man whispers words in a different language, his nose almost touching beak when he places it gently down. The bird lies on its back, breathing in, out, in, out. When the man takes his hands away from its round body it does not struggle to its feet. It stays pale, calm, wings make light trails in the sand.

The scruffy man sings softly to the goose, never taking his eyes from it. The bird plays at being dead, transfixed. In a second it is over. A flash of silver in the firelight. Not a sound as the knife bares down on the shell neck of the goose. Little black specks of ash cling to Amy's damp skin, as she runs across stones and sand, freckled in violet bird-blood.

Amy is lobster-hot, shivering. She has not had time to dream. Beneath the door is a chink of light, the whish of running water. Her father must be up. Making tea, taking a shower. Stillness outside tells her it is still yesterday. Not yet time to get up.

'Dad? Dad?' Amy slips slightly. There is a pool of water on the floor; she follows the light to the bathroom. The door is ajar, the sound of coughing, gargling. The room smells of vomit and auld lang syne.

'You all right?'

On the floor, the peacock-paisley of her father's dressing gown is a crumpled heap; he crouches on all fours, leaning over the toilet. He turns, holds his hand level, gesturing his daughter away from his prone form. The cold tap runs on. Kneeling, he moves to the sink, ducks his head, his face grey, crumpled as a used tissue as he suckles from the tap. His back arches, as he wretches, convulses.

'Shall I go get a doctor?' The body shakes its head. For a moment he pulls his head away from the flow.

'No. Too much sun.' He swallows, presses his hand to his chest and scoops up water with both hands .

'Dad, don't drink the water it'll make you bad.' Amy cries, she doesn't know anything.

What is the matter with her father? He smells funny, for a moment she wants to run. Out there, she imagines trying to explain how ill her father is in hand gestures to snake-eyed strangers. Thinking on wet feet she turns. On the counter she lifts bottles to fetch to her father. In the open-door half-light she can see two water bottles are empty, and another has spilt. The bottle on its side ebbs onto the lino and across to the carpet. Amy picks it up, places it beside the empties.

The water tablets. She lifts a bottle and fills it with tap water, pops a tablet out of the plastic and drops in purity. Then she picks up another. The empty bottle is cold, glass, heavy in her hand. Her fingers graze the label. She holds the empty to the light. That smell. A picture of a stag. The word *Scottish*.

Amy buys squash when he has sucked all the rivers dry. Her father lies under a white sheet on a lounger, the cotton flickering lightly as he snores. Placing change in her purse, her fingers touch neat folds of paper with her mother's handwriting, In case of emergency.

Amy dials, six rings. I'll give it ten then hang up she decides.

'Hello? Hello?' It is her mother's voice, efficient as a newsreader. A voice reserved for people she cannot see, people who might get the better of her. A far away kind of voice.

'Amy, it's you? Can you hear me? Is everything OK? Are you there?'

Amy has not yet answered.

'Is he taking care of you?'

Without knowing what she is going to say, she opens her mouth.

Shauna Mackay
Hush

The voices in my father's head were pranksters. They had him run naked through the park. I can imagine these voices having faces. Fleshy faces with twisted smirks and I see them doing little bobbing victory dances in celebration of their foxy supremacy. I am sad that they did not allow him a dignified madness.

We were a family of four. Esme, my older sister, led a vital, tireless life. In our shared attic room with twin divans, I would lie, stomach down, in my classroom-crumpled clothes and watch, drowsily, as she performed exquisite acts of self-enhancement. Her neat body, in white bra and pants, would bow down close to the dressing-table mirror as if to hear a whispered secret from a friend. Raising one sleek eyebrow, she stroked, with a steady hand, velvet mascara onto silk lashes. Finally, having wrapped herself in a dress and a mist of powder and spray, she would painstakingly grease her pouted mouth. Esme was a collector of lipstick — she loved it. Later, left alone in the buttery afternoon light that shafted across the bedroom, I would investigate her treasured stockpile.

Esme side-stepped the mess that was our homelife with a poised unconcern. I was rarely allowed in close but the day dad painted the backyard vermilion she did put out a sisterly hand. Everything was red.

Walls
Ground
Window

Toilet Door
Coalhouse Door
Back Door
Battered Bin
Dinted Lid (Of Bin)

Everything dripped. Little blood streams. Everywhere. Indoors, mother wept little streams of her own and waited for the doctor. We sat in the back lane and picked at the hot tar. The determined digging in of fingers not lessening the guilt I felt at worrying what the neighbours would be saying this time.

Esme broke the silence. 'He could've done it pink.'

'Why?'

'Well, it's a much nicer colour and besides, you know what they say, 'pink makes the boys wink'. She said this with a frenzied twitching of her right eye. We started to giggle and didn't stop until I got wheezy.

Esme liked boys. She lost herself in a busy promiscuity. I would follow her to the park — to the trees and bushes that acted as leafy cloaks — to the boys who all looked the same. I like to think she was glad I was around the night the stabbing poker pains came and she miscarried onto the turquoise swirls of our bedroom carpet. Taking a pair of fresh, folded knickers from her drawer, I scooped up the pulpy stickiness and silently tiptoed to the yard where I dropped it into the bin. The battered red bin. After washing the carpet with shampoo I crawled back into my still-warm bed. Esme seemed well the next day and I knew not to mention anything. It could have been a dream but for a stain on a turquoise swirl.

There was a cyclical nature to dad's illness. It reared every fourth year and was heralded by sleep. He would take to the settee and we would know that long bus journeys lay ahead. Travel-sick journeys on itchy seats to see our father in the hospital on top of the hill. Long corridors, foody smells and disinfectant. Plastic seats and fruit bowls. Ladies in crimplene skirts with dough-like cheeks and loose, flabby lips scurrying to the tuck shop with dirty handbags. Once, a tall man with gravestone teeth walked round taking photographs of everyone with a newspaper picture of a camera. Click, click went his huge forefinger. Doo lally click.

Somewhere along the way my mother turned to stone and I turned to books. Boarding school stories were my favourite. The brown socks and plaits — the predictability.

I remember hearing mother say to dad one time, 'Our sex life is nil.' I strained to hear an answer, a contradiction, but he said not one solitary word in response. In childhood we overhear things we do not fully understand but know to be important. We never forget and years later assimilate it as an adult when it becomes a new fresh stab. Parents beware.

I was twelve, and Esme sixteen, when mother left. She said, 'Girls, be good now — I'll come and get you when I'm sorted.' A month later while she was still 'getting sorted' my father hanged himself in a moment of cold sanity. We were taken from school by an aunt whose mouth was set into an 'O' shape with shock — goldfish-like. Back to mother in the flat where she sat with eyes like brown jasper. A round stone in a square box with a lid on top.

I left home on a coach the day John Lennon got shot. I was seventeen. I write birthdays and Christmas but haven't been back. Yoko's nearly an old woman now and I'm doing OK.

I met Billy when he came into Dario's five, six years ago. It was late on a Wednesday night so the place was quiet. When I took his order I was aware of every blink and lip movement I made, because it was an instant thing. I looked at him and it was like I already knew him. The body under the checked shirt, inside the jeans, the spikiness of the short hair on his neck when rubbed up the wrong way, the strength of his hands — carpenter's hands. I dropped the bill onto the table after he'd eaten and he touched my arm. I can still feel that touch now.

'What time are you off?' he said.

'About twelve-thirty... Why?'

'I don't suppose there's any chance of walking you back?'

He smiled and my stomach flipped. I couldn't believe his nerve and then I couldn't believe mine when I smiled back and said, 'You haven't got far to walk. I live in the bed-sit two doors down, it comes with the job.'

A long time after that first night I told Billy, 'My childhood was like a dot-to-dot puzzle. I followed each step carefully, deliberately, but it ended up jagged and sad. I know if I could have another go I'd do it with a lighter touch — more casually like Esme — and it would be better.'

He said, 'Go on ... cry... cry for your father. Don't be scared.'

I said, 'Do you know, when my aunt told me he was dead all I could think about was that she had a mouth like a fish.'

'And you fed her aunts' eggs I suppose.'

'Ha, ha — but isn't it weird how the saddest events in life are prevented from being completely noble by some small ridiculous aspect?'

'You mean like Elvis died having a shit.' He stooped in front of me and made an appropriate face. I pushed him away and carried on.

'The guilt stops you acknowledging the funny side,' I said. Because it's true. It builds up into a virtually uncontrollable guffaw in the throat. We are all walking around with a suppressed guffaw that's ready to jump out like a jack-in-the-box if we ever relax our throats.

My mother rang me at work yesterday. She spoke loudly, competing with clattering plates and Dario's singing.

'Come and see us... It's been too long.'

I thought on my feet. 'I don't know, mam ... I don't think I can get the time off work, we're really...'

'Please... Esme's moved back in.'

'Oh?'

'...Bring Billy, I should meet him.'

'We'll try and get up at Christmas,' I hedged.

'...Please,' she said. 'Christmas is six months away.'

I had to relent. 'OK, I'll see what I can do.'

She paused. She wanted to say something other than goodbye.

'You know your father's madness was nothing to do with me.'

'I know, mam... I know that...' I put the receiver down and realised that I had come to understand that what she said was true. Madness is its own master.

So I'm on a coach again — nearly there. Billy's doing the crossword and I'm looking out of the breath-covered window seeing the park. Esme's park. Kids are splashing round the paddling pool and I wonder what sort of father Billy will be. Too soon and I'm tapping on my mother's door. She's standing there. Her hair is different — shorter, thinner. I drop my bags and take some boxes out from one of them. I hand over the chocolates, filling the space between us and leave Billy and her to make greeting noises. Shy, over-polite. I walk to the door of the small living room and watch Esme from behind. She is sitting on the settee, alone. Her head is turned slightly to the left and I notice she is nodding as if deep in conversation. Tiny, frantic nods. Whispered secrets from a friend. Red clouds burst in my head and flood my brain. Her lips move in a hissing communion and I want to scream but know I will not. I say her name instead. Like a sigh — 'Esme'. She jumps up like lightning and comes to me. The sleek eyebrows have grown spidery. I say I've brought her a present and press the box into her hands. She opens it, revealing the twelve small rectangles inside arranged in rows of four. The mirror in the lid shows her pleasure and together, reflected, we look down at the flesh and blood colours of the lipstick.

Joe Quinn

Tobhta an Da Mhail
The Ruin with Two Rents

The dues were extorted twice,
The rent and the seed corn,
But this did not suffice,
Now runrig and croft were gone.

A force, with Factor, Sheriff,
At McDonald's order,
Punched a hole in the roof,
Dowsed the hearth with water.

Crofters fought with the polis
Who smashed furniture once
Women threw pots of piss
And swore their defiance.

But they were not strong enough.
Minister and wife stood by
As they were dragged off
Crying, towards the sea.

Common the image of grim men,
Staring out of the stern
And next to them the women,
A shawl covering the wean.

This was a last goodbye
To little Malacleit or
Solas, many to die
On Ontario's frozen shore.

Peter Baker

Coach Touch

a slender arm   the right one
white   with its dainty hand
is raised above that seat
to reach and push in the nozzle
which stops the flow of air
just as perhaps those same
fingers will fondly be found and pressed
to a kiss from the lips of a lover
of the girl whose arm it is
gone now from the glance
of an anxious fellow passenger
who extends a wavering paw
over his seat to the valve O
through which he'd feel her soft breath

Modern Love

And so they both go out this afternoon
Together (having been thus for one year
Six months two weeks and five days) to Ikea
M for a change driving the Audi saloon
Nicely lunched with F scanning the Sundays
Stopping en route at Paradise for a new
Patio lamp and while there just a few
Odds and sods that take the fancy (fun days
Flashing the plastic!) F remarking
Apropos of nothing how the Seychelles
Would make a welcome break again (sea-shells
Embedded in the stucco!) M parking
Up the car then switching off sat quite still
(It was three fourteen, the ninth) utters low
My soul is arrowy to the light in you
And slumps forehead-first on the steering-wheel

Kevan Ogden
Grief

She was in the kitchen, turning from the table to the sink, when she saw him. He was standing in the yard making faces at her through the window.

First there was surprise and oddly, when she remembered, embarrassment — a sense that by her thoughts she had let him down.

He pushed open the stiff back door, wiped his feet on the mat and plonked a carrier bag onto the table Emma had just cleared. It was the solidness of the sounds that struck her.

'Just some pies,' he said. 'Corned beef and potato, mince and a sausage roll.'

She looked hard at him. But could not say it. A droplet hung from the beak of his nose. He drew the back of his hand across his face and it had gone.

'Any tea on the go?'

Behind him the door was still open. Cold air pushed its way in. Emma felt it on her bare arms. The hairs were bristling. She pushed against the door and heard the catch snap into the mortise.

He sat down in his coat as he always had and Emma, switching back into the habit she'd so recently sloughed off, brought out the raffia mats, the small plates and the knives. She watched him pull the paper bags from the carrier, tearing them down the middle so the pastries lay side by side exposed. Golden. Automatically she brought brown sauce from the fridge.

'That tea,' he said, 'I'm dying for a drink.'

It made Emma feel like he was toying with her. She looked at him and cleared her throat but still couldn't speak. The clock on the wall waited awhile — its finger eventually flicking into the black mark of the next minute.

'Here, look out!'

Suddenly he was on his feet, the fabric of his coat squeaking as it rubbed up against the wooden units. Emma felt herself bustled aside, sandwiched between his body and the kitchen door. Sniffing, she tasted the moth-balls on his clothes, the coconut oil he rubbed into his scalp every morning. She had already pulled the cosy from the teapot and three of her fingers were hooked through its handle. A membrane of catarrh seemed to be stretched across her throat but she managed to speak. Her voice came through thickly.

'It'll be cold now.'

'Let's feel it,' he said.

She felt his firm grasp and a tug as he cupped his hands around the pot's earthenware belly, testing its temperature. There was a brief contact with the warm flesh of his fingers.

'It'll do,' he said. 'Plenty warm enough. Just get it poured out will you?'

When she brought the cup to him she saw he had taken a knife and had perfectly halved the pies. Flakes of pastry had spilled onto the tablecloth.

'Busy?'

She opened her mouth, found it hard to speak again, wondered how it would come out, wondered what would come out.

'No, I'm not'— and she named him — 'dad.'

'And Martin and the kids?'

'Fine. They're fine.'

'It's cold out there.'

'Yes,' she said.

She sat opposite him. Sliced the pies and raised the cut portions to her lips. Closing her lips down onto the tines of the fork she drew off the food. In her mouth the potato and the pastry was softly collapsing. She looked into her cup. Globules of fat from the milk circled on the surface of the tepid tea.

'That clematis needs pruning!'

'Yes dad.'

Turning from him to look out into the yard she saw its tendrils had wound themselves around the cable coming down from the aerial.

'It'll have that wire off the wall.'

'We cut it back every year,' she said, 'but it keeps climbing.'

'Up to the light,' he said, then thumping his chest with his closed fist: 'I think I'm getting a touch of heartburn.'

'It's the flaky pastry,' she said. 'You never learn.'

He rummaged around in his pockets — pulled out a loose mint covered in fluff, popped it into his mouth long enough for the saliva to loosen the detritus and spat into his grimy handkerchief.

'Dad!' she said. It seemed he could still disgust her.

And the thin finger moved into another minute.

'Look,' he said, heaving himself up and brushing the flakes lodged in his clothes onto the floor. 'I've some sorting out to do down the flat. I'll see you later on.'

'You're not angry with me?' She had to ask.

'Why should I be?' he asked. 'It's just I've left the place in a mess.'

There was a ball of meat lodged at the corner of his mouth. She dared herself to reach across and scrape it away with her nail. She touched stiff skin and whiskers. He winced.

'Sorry,' she said.

'It's all right,' he said.

She looked at him and sighed.

'I'll pop in tomorrow love. Okay?'

He turned — winked. She saw him to the door, wanted to see him to the gate at least, but of course she couldn't.

He called to see her every day after that and always around dinner. Usually he'd bring food but just now and then he'd let her whisk something up. She'd do him simple stuff like scrambled egg, cheese on toast, soup from a tin, or sardines — their tragic silver bodies laid out on toast. After dinner they'd sit and talk.

He was a browser, a voracious reader, moving between rooms consuming sentences from opened letters, forgotten newspapers, picking up paperbacks and folding them back on themselves. She didn't say anything though she knew he was quietly breaking their spines. He'd read random extracts out loud to her while she washed up the dinner things.

'*Listen to this...once again quality gives way to quantity so that although vastly more pleasuresome to the palate Langley Gage is nowhere near as heavy cropping as Invicta.*'

It comforted her to hear him ramble on.

'The diver can be recognised by its plaintive howl like some strange lake creature mourning the death of a loved one.'

Once though — it had been a close thing — she had had to rush over to take from him the pile of cards he had idly picked up from the top of the piano. Her heart thudding she had tried to make her sudden reaction appear casual.

'I've been meaning to throw those out,' she said, twisting the sombre stack from his grasp so he wouldn't learn the truth. And as soon as he had gone she did just that, tearing them into halves then quarters and eighths and dropping them into the bin.

It was the Tuesday of the second week of his visits that she heard the front door bell. Her dad was watering the geranium that she kept on the kitchen windowsill. She closed the door on him and went through to the front. Bright winter sunlight sluiced the passage. Brought in coal smoke from the chimney next door but one. Emma's sister filled the doorway.

'I've just been looking at curtains in the market. There's not the...' She tried to step forward but there was nowhere she could put down her foot. Emma was blocking her way.

'What's the matter?'

'What do you mean?'

'Well aren't I gonna get in?'

'Got the insurance man in,' said Emma

'S'okay I'll just wait in the front room.'

'It'll take a while.'

'I am able to entertain myself you know.'

'I'd rather you didn't.' Emma was going dizzy. She'd already been too long at the door. Above Cathy's head the pale blue sky was threatening to suck her up.

'Look you know I can't stand...'

'Then let me in.'

'I can't.'

There seemed to be a moment of darkness. A temporary loss of consciousness. Something was constricting her breathing. When Emma came round she found she was propping herself up against the wall, staring at the embossed leaves of her wallpaper. She felt sick. The door had been slammed by someone because she was behind it listening to Cathy's voice saying 'You need help you do girl.'

'Who was that?' said her dad when she got back. He was plucking dead leaves from the thickening stem of the plant. It gave off an earthy smell of potatoes.

'Feller selling washcloths.'

'You could have got me one, I need a new one.'

'I don't like buying from people like that,' she said, keeping the lie going. 'They never seem genuine.'

'You need to take a cutting,' he said, 'this has about had it. You need to take it from there.'

Emma leaned forward into his minty breath, watched his dirty fingernail flick at a leaf juncture.

'Dip it in rooting powder. Tuck it into some John Innes. That way you never lose the plant.'

She looked at him — at the grey in his moustache — at the reflection of light in his blue eyes.

'Dad,' she said.

'Yes?' he asked.

But she lost her nerve.

'You need a shave.'

'My razor's kaput,' he said.

The weekend came and her father stayed away. Emma wasn't surprised. She understood that it was because he knew Martin would be there. Friends called round on the Friday night. Emma fixed them a stir-fry, staring out at herself in the black mirror of the kitchen window. When she sat down at the table with them she laughed and chatted and wished they would go home.

On Saturday, Martin took her to *The Cherry Orchard*, pulling into a disabled bay to let her out and then driving off to find somewhere to park. The auditorium was small enough for her to stay in control but when the audience laughed at Feers Nikolayevich calling out from the locked house she felt the slow slippage of warm tears down her cheeks, tasted them when they reached the corners of her mouth. In the slow mumbling shuffle of the crowd as it left she kept her head down and hoped no-one had noticed her.

Sunday irritated Emma. Its hours dragged on. She made the dinner and ironed and half-watched a film set in America in the Depression. And when she found herself without anything to do, she wandered into Simon's room so she could look down into the empty yard.

When Monday came she found she was smiling again. As usual she got up first and prepared Martin's breakfast. She waited for him, impatiently. He got up late — seemed unable to organise himself. He took his time over breakfast, popped in a second piece of toast and sat back unwashed in his vest and jogging pants. The night sweat on his skin leaked into the kitchen and made her feel sick.

'You're going to be late,' she said irritably.

He stretched and she saw the damp black hairs in his arm-pits releasing their pungency.

'Not going.'

She looked at him.

'What?'

'I'm taking the day off,' he smiled. 'We're going to celebrate.'

She was quietly panicking. Her palms felt clammy and aggravated.

'Celebrate what?'

'Oh come on Emma — only the wedding anniversary.'

Emma looked across at the calendar. Snow on the Seven Sisters of Kintail. He was right. They were already in December. Her heart sank.

'I'm not sure I feel like it.'

'Emma!'

'How can I go outside?' she whined.

'You won't have to, will you? It'll be door to door.'

'Where?'

He had booked a hotel in the Lakes. 'What was the point?' she'd asked, tears starting in her eyes again. He said the views from the windows were superb. 'I really don't feel like it,' she'd complained. He told her it was already paid for.

All the way he played tapes he'd copied from the vinyls they had bought each other as twenty year olds back in college. Neil Young, Joni Mitchell, Leonard Cohen, Dylan. Their words smeared across Emma's ears. She looked out of the car window at blocks of matter that were cars, at the random code of hedge — sign — tree — building. She looked at the icy sky and she looked at her watch.

Martin reached out to the radio and pressed a switch. There was a wad of silence that made Emma turn her head.

'What's this between you and Cath then?' he asked, his eyes still focused on the road ahead.

She'd been in touch then! Emma could imagine the conversation. She tried to stay calm.

'Oh you know Cath — seeing insults where there aren't any.'

'You didn't say anything to me about an insurance man.'

'It wasn't important, that's why?'

'Which company? Cath said there was no car parked outside.'

'Oh for God's sake!' She suddenly saw her father standing in the yard, staring into an empty house. She wanted to be with him. 'Look just turn round, drop me off, and go to work will you?'

'I've taken out leave! I've paid for the hotel.'

'I'll give you the money!' It sounded ridiculous to her as she said it — she had no money of her own but she wouldn't give up — 'Just turn round! I want to go back home!'

'For God's sake!' he spat. A slip-road was right there on his left. He swerved into it. A driver behind them jabbed at his horn.

'Just drop me off somewhere. There's nothing to stop you going.'

Martin revved up to the roundabout at the top of the slipway, slammed on his brakes and waited for a space.

'Oh yeah,' he snarled and hit the accelerator. The engine ground along in second for too long. 'I'm going to spend a weekend in a hotel on my own! Sign myself in as Mister Sad Bastard!'

'I'm just not up to it!'

'Your Cath's coped!'

'I'm not our Cath!'

'Sod it!' he shouted, smacking the indicator arm up but missing the turning back south. Swinging the car around the roundabout he did a complete circuit — and then a second — and a third. Emma found herself being thrown up against the side of the car then back the other way against Martin's body.

'Martin!'

'What?'

'Stop being stupid!'

He seemed to be about to clock-up a fourth circuit when he suddenly swung out and down the road to take them north again.

'We're going. I'm not wasting a hundred quid!'
A man in a van trying to come up on his right was mouthing and waving his hands around. Martin blew him a fierce kiss, the man hit his horn and Martin accelerated away.

'This is stupid!' said Emma.

'I agree!' said Martin and pressed the power button on the radio.

A big blue sign for Kendal came up. They drove past it. Fat drops of rain came down on the windscreen. The wipers went to work.

A winding drive of crushed stone through a tunnel of rhododendron and sycamore brought them to a wide-fronted hotel of grey-blue rock. Martin parked up and opened the door. Emma rushed quickly inside. The foyer was dark with panels, heavy furniture and a staircase straight from the set of a costume drama. A fire squandered its heat, occasionally breathing smoke into the room. Wood smoke — and polish. A chandelier dangled from the ceiling and glum men and women in period costume hung from the walls conscious that they were being looked at.

Their bedroom was similarly dark. Emma went to the window. Pushed her nose up against the double-glazing, felt heat come up at her from the bulky coils of the radiator. Outside bare beds stuffed with sleeping flowers, a path, steps, a lawn. Then a fringe of rhododendrons, a field, a wind-creased lake, a scree slope crested with snow and finally the sky.

'Told you,' said Martin, coming up behind her and squeezing her in at the shoulders.

Downstairs at dinner they were adopted by a middle-aged couple. Walkers with weathered faces. Over the years winds had buffeted them, the veins in their cheeks had popped as they'd strained up hills and the rain had washed away the man's hair. They were the old guard shunning Gore Tex, sticking with leather, Harris Tweed and oil skins.

'We wouldn't dream of coming here in the summer! Far too crowded,' said the woman — Eleanor. 'We take ourselves off to somewhere exotic then. You'd be surprised how even on tourist islands like Majorca or Tenerife there's out of the way places where you hardly see a soul.'

Emma's mouth made a smile. Martin *mmmed* interestedly.

'You walkers?' asked the man.

'Emma's got a problem at present,' said Martin.

Emma looked at him but it was too late for Martin to retreat.

The eyebrows of the couple went up asking the same question twice.

'Agoraphobic,' Emma, head down, heard him say. 'Temporarily, we hope!'

The woman smiled.

'Seems strange to come out here then.'

Emma raised her head. 'That's exactly what I said.'

'Oh dear, treading on toes? Change of subject time Clive!'

They spent the afternoon clocking up miles and scenery. Emma risked a sprint into a café up in the clouds where she ordered scones with rum butter. Outside soggy sheep blundered around. It was dark when they got back.

At night in the bar the woman came over again.

'Been up Skiddaw this afternoon. Thought we'd risk it. The rocks are polished by so many tourist boots that it's almost as dangerous in summer as in winter. Took the ice picks though. Might seem a bit Himalayan but you really do need them in places.'

Emma excused herself.

Eleven. She lay in the dark and listened to the night. The wind slid down the valleys between the fells and slapped the hotel around the face. She slid into sleep and the wind became waves beating at the prow of a plunging steamer. Around one o'clock she woke to footsteps and suppressed laughter. A young couple. Giddy with drink or love they moved up the staircase and a door opened above Emma's head. The wind surged against the house again and Emma, her eyes glossy in the matt blackness of the room, remembered the cuffing and swell of the sea as she rode in her grandfather's tug. It became her breathing and she rose and fell with it — a child again. Around her the creaking of wood — the straining of the engine. Salt was on her lips and the cold air forcing itself into her open mouth. Her shoe touched seaweed strewn on the deck. She slipped and jerked awake. The creaking was above her now regular and insistent — short vowels — private noises gone public.

She turned to Martin. A corpse's head in the bed beside her. Tonight he had not asked her; he had not tried to take her hand in his to place it onto his body. But soon she would be expected to admit it was becoming a problem. Martin would call in the professionals. Already there had been arguments:

'It can't go on like this you know! It happens to other people — they get over it!'

Dropping into Emma's head came the sudden idea that she would go outside. Martin didn't stir, didn't feel the bed rise as she left it, didn't hear her shuffling among her clothes. Wrapped in her fleece Emma pulled out the key on its heavy plastic fob, eased the door open and shut, and moved down the stairs. It occurred to her that the outer door might be alarmed but she risked it, clenching her teeth against the sound that never came. Stepping out she prepared for an assault by the wind but there was no wind — the bulk of the house was outfacing it and the back was sheltered. Emma took a deep breath. The cold swarmed around her. She chuffed warm air up out of her lungs. And waited for the space to turn her dizzy.

Nothing happened. Around her the light from the sliver of moon bounced back from the rubbery leaves of the rhododendrons. Her feet crunched the gravel.

Lifting her face to the sky Emma saw a wealth of stars. She looked into them, waiting as they slowly came together into patterns. The cool still air bathed her body and she closed her eyes, remembering the night after her mother had died when her father had sat with her in her bedroom. 'Look!' he'd said, his finger reaching out through the open window and fixing onto a single star. 'Look! That one there! That's your mam!' And Emma the child had stared then, till her eyes hurt, at her mother who'd taken up her place in the night sky.

She let her eyelids open slowly like buds. Space was stuffed with stars and she no longer recognised her mother up there. Then she gasped, startled. A star had suddenly peeled itself from its constellation, was careering away across the sky. It took a full two seconds before she realised it was merely a plane — a tubeful of cramped humans up there coming back from somewhere exotic — tee-shirted and shorted to shiver soon in the cold northern air.

The next morning she shocked Martin by stepping outside. She walked over to a bench, sat down and stretched out her legs.

'That's marvellous darling!' he simpered. 'A first step to recovery.'

On Wednesday Emma prepared a carbonara for her father but he didn't come. She stood by the window and waited all afternoon. Finally she went out to the gate and looked down the street. By four o'clock she couldn't wait any longer. Pulling on her coat she walked along the road and turned into his avenue. Coming to his flat she inserted the key and turned it. It was empty but she could smell him. She walked into the bedroom but he wasn't there. She slumped to the bare carpet, propping herself against the wall where his bed had been and drew her coat around her.

With Christmas came the kids back from college bringing their washing and the bits and pieces they couldn't leave in their flats. They filled up the house with their bodies and their concerns.

Around ten o'clock on Christmas morning she half-heartedly began the dinner.

Popping into the front room she found the kids flopping in chairs in the sleepy heat. They had slid easily back into childhood, tearing at their presents and whooping.

'Why hasn't Auntie Cath come round?' Simon asked, pocketing the envelope of notes she'd posted through the door.

Emma shrugged. She saw Martin glance at her.

She was okay with the turkey, the carrots, the parsnip and the roast potatoes but she cried into the meat loaf, her tears blending in with the sausage meat, the chestnuts and the onions.

Carole came in, heading for the backyard with a cigarette to smoke outside. She put her arms around her mum.

'Grandad always liked the meat loaf, didn't he?' she said. 'It was always his favourite.'

'Yes,' she said, the tears in her eyes making the window wobble.

It was his recipe.

Emma went upstairs and got a chair. She placed it under the light fitting and stood on it. From the top of the wardrobe she produced a parcel wrapped in red and gold. She read her own handwriting bold and blue on the dangling label. *To dad with all my love Emma* and then a smattering of Xs. She snapped it off, screwed it into her palm and binned it. Stepping down she went to her bedside cabinet, brought out a virgin label and wrote Martin's name on it.

Downstairs she handed him the present, kissed him dryly on the cheek.

'Is this a hint by any chance?' he asked, drawing his fingers through his beard and looking down at the electric razor.

'Happy Christmas,' she said.

under the bridge...

(1: 1st Year of the MA; 2: 2nd Year; G: Graduate)

Peter Baker, a Southerner who trained as a biologist, now lives in central Newcastle (an feelin reet canny te be gannin te skeul agyain.) Publications include *Mayday* (Ferry Press), *Cracks on the Sun Terrace* (Rivelin Press) and 999 (Idle Pirate Editions). He edited *Skylight* magazine and was, for some time, associate editor of Redbeck Press. **(1)**

John Barfoot has been writing stories for as long as he can remember. Some have been published, most recently in *The Printer's Devil* and *The Unexpected Pond* (Route, 2000). **(G)**

Celia Bryce is a short-story writer, singer-songwriter and children's storyteller. She runs writing workshops in Tyneside and is a regular fiction contributor to *Woman's Weekly*. She was a runner-up in the Fish Prize 2000; winner of the Marches Literary Award in 1999; winner of Midland Exposure Competition in 1999; second prize winner in the *Cork Literary Review* Competition 1998; second prize winner in the Matthew Prichard Award in 1998. 'Sheets' has been previously published in *Cork Literary Review* 1998. **(G)**

Chris Coles is a sometime sculptor, playwright, carpenter and painter of a mean mackerel who has washed up in the North-East and fathered three Geordie children. **(1)**

Philippa Collingwood feels she peaked with 'Instructions for Rollerblading,' which was first published in *The Blue Room Anthology* and then in *The Independent*. She has now turned to songwriting. **(G)**

Bob Cooper has won four *Pamphlet Competitions* in four years. *Drinking Up Time* (Redbeck Press 1997) and *The Ideal Overcoat* (Jackson's Arms 1998) were each written during his MA. His latest book, *Making Poems*, is published by Incredible Press. He lives in Newcastle but is about to move to Middlesbrough. **(G)**

Joanna Curtis is a teacher who writes in her spare moments. **(2)**

Marie Dobson is relieved to have rediscovered her ability to write prose as well as poetry. She is planning to become a creative-writing tutor. **(1)**

Josephine Fagan works part-time as a doctor. She has worked as a medic in South America (which provided her with the inspiration for 'The Taste of Honey') and in Australia. She has had two medical texts published and collaborated on several comedy reviews. **(1)**

Adam Fish has had work published in *Sepia, Marginalia, First Time* and *Dandelion*. He has performed at Origins, The Voice Box and the Beatniks Boogaloo in Newcastle and also in Edinburgh. **(1)**

Chrissie Glazebrook's poems were previously published in *Writing Women*. Her first novel, *The Madolescents*, will be published by Arrow in 2001, to be followed by a sequel in 2002. **(G)**

Caron Henderson lives in Sunderland. She writes poetry and prose, some of which she has read at the Blue Room, and is busy working on her first novel. **(2)**

Eileen Jones has always lived in the North-East. She has been writing poetry for a long time, but with more regularity over the past year. She has read at the Blue Room, had poems published in the *Red Herring*, and has a poem in a forthcoming Iron Press anthology. **(1)**

Pru Kitching left Weardale to go to drama school. After finishing there she went to London, married a painter, then left England to see the world. Quitting the world, she returned to Weardale to be the writer she always should have been. **(2)**

Janine Langley-McCann grew up in Leeds and has lived and worked in the North-East for seven years. A mother of four, she abandoned education at fifteen, only recently returning, initially to college, then to university. The MA in Creative Writing will be her first-ever qualification. Previous work published includes 'Clingy,' in *Hasty*, and 'Down the Bull,' in *Braquemard*. 'A cake fit for a skinbird' was first published in the journal *Lateral Moves*. **(2)**

Karen Laws has had work published in *Hasty*, and a ten-minute play performed at the Blue Room. **(1)**

Valerie Laws is a graduate in English and Maths, disabled, and an associate editor of Iron Press. She is also a prize-winning poet, published in many magazines and anthologies and in a joint collection with Kitty Fitzgerald, *For Crying Out Loud* (Iron). She is the editor of the forthcoming anthology, *Star Trek-the Poems*. **(2)**

Shauna Mackay is married with three daughters and lives in Blyth. Her short story in this collection has previously been published in *Sunday People*. In 2000 she won a Northern Promise Award. She is working on a novel. **(2)**

Jo McCullock was born in Birkenhead, Merseyside. She currently teaches video production at the University of Sunderland. **(2)**

Brighid Morrigan is currently working on her first novel. **(2)**

Jo Morris is a twenty nine year old mother of two, and would-be writer, living in Newcastle. **(2)**

Patrick Murphy, while waiting for redemption, is busy turning a life of crime into a life of rhyme. He is currently developing a performance of his work, 'Perfecting the Heat.' **(1)**

Kriss Nichol lives in Blyth after having done VSO work in Nepal. She now works as a supply teacher. **(1)**

Kevan Ogden, after early success with poems on radio and television, largely abandoned poetry to write five novels which were 'witty and horrid', 'terrific reads' — and apparently unpublishable. Short-listed for the 1996 Northern Radio Playwright of the Year, his most recent work can be found in *Erotic Review* and other non-pc publications, usually under a pseudonym. **(2)**

Matthew Pacey did an English degree at the University of Northumbria. He has read at the Blue Room and is currently putting together a collection of short stories, revolving around three characters living in a small, working-class town, much like the one he grew up in. **(2)**

Gary Player is from Edinburgh but is now an adopted Geordie. He is working on his first novel, which revolves around the world of drink and madness. **(1)**

Chris Powell teaches Performing Arts and is just beginning to get her work published in national magazines. **(2)**

Joe Quinn lives in Gateshead, where he teaches. He is currently writing a sequence of poems on the Western Isles. **(1)**

Angela Readman's poetry has appeared in several magazines. Her short story,

'On a Clear Blue Day,' appeared in *Unhinged* (February 2000) and she has another short story forthcoming in *London Magazine*. In 2000 she won a New Writing North and Northern Arts Promise Award. **(2)**

Marlynn Rosario has had work published in variety of small presses, including *London Magazine*, *Orbis*, *Smiths Knoll*, *Other Place*. She has had work published in *The Blue Room Anthology* and in *Wild Cards* (Virago). She was a winner in the Poetry Business Book and Pamphlet Competition in 1997 and a runner up in the National Poetry Competition 1999. Her first collection is to be published by Diamond Twig Press in Autumn 2000. **(G)**

Gareth Rowe was born and brought up in Liverpool. He studied for his first degree at Durham and now lives and works in Newcastle upon Tyne. **(2)**

Andrea Russell was a journalist in Canada before moving to York in 1997. She is now working on her first novel. **(2)**

Liz Sampson was born and brought up in Ireland. She has lived in England for thirty-five years, twenty-seven of those in the North-East, which she loves. She never wrote a thing until she was fifty. She is married with two sons, two daughters, and three grandchildren. **(2)**

Penny Smith is the Course Leader for the MA in Creative Writing at the University of Northumbria. Under the name Penny Sumner she has had two novels published, *The End of April* (The Women's Press, 1993) and *Crosswords* (The Women's Press, 1995). Her short stories have appeared in a number of publications in Britain and the United States and she is the editor of *Brought to Book: Murderous Stories from the Literary World* (The Women's Press, 1998).

Sue Vickerman used to write articles for *The Guardian* and *Times Educational Supplement* but now writes poetry and short stories. Her stories have appeared in *Wild Cards* (Virago, 1999) and *The Unexpected Pond* (Route, 2000). She is working on a novel and looking for a publisher for her first short-story collection. **(G)**

Katherine Zeserson is a singer, community musician and music educator. Over the past three years she has started to see herself as a writer and is currently working on her first novel. She has a teenage son. **(2)**

MA Creative Writing

One year full-time or two years part-time.
Starts September 2000.

This highly successful MA allows you to specialise in either poetry or prose, or to work in both forms. This is a practical degree, designed for people who wish to become published writers, as well as for those involved in the teaching of creative writing or in other areas of the writing industry.

Teaching sessions of three hours take place during the evenings, twice a week for full-time students and once a week for part-time. The sessions are usually made up of a workshop, followed by a seminar.

The writing workshops, which are the backbone of the degree, provide you with a stimulating and supportive environment in which to learn from the work of others, whilst at the same time developing your own voice as a writer. There are also seminar classes on Contemporary Literature, the Writing Industry (including Editing), and the Writer as Tutor.

Applications close end of August 2000.

Other courses on offer are: MA Cultural History; PG Dip Arts Management; MA Conservation of Fine Art; MA History of Ideas.

**For further details please contact the School of Humanities on:
0191 227 4995**

UNIVERSITY of NORTHUMBRIA at NEWCASTLE